ENDGAME

ENDGAME

The Blueprint for Victory in the War on Terror

Lt. General Thomas McInerney
USAF (Ret.)

Maj. General Paul Vallely
US Army (Ret.)

Since 1947
REGNERY
PUBLISHING, INC.
An Eagle Publishing Company • Washington, DC

Library of Congress Cataloging-in-Publication Data

McInerney, Thomas.
  Endgame : the blueprint for victory in the war on terror / Thomas McInerney and Paul E. Vallely.
      p. cm.
  ISBN 0-89526-066-2 (hardcover)
  ISBN 0-89526-000-X (paperback)
  1. War on Terrorism, 2001–   I. Vallely, Paul E. II. Title.
  HV6432.M387 2004
  973.931—dc22

                                                          2004004909

First paperback edition published in 2006

Published in the United States by
Regnery Publishing, Inc.
An Eagle Publishing Company
One Massachusetts Avenue, NW
Washington, DC 20001
Visit us at www.regnery.com

Distributed to the trade by
National Book Network
4720-A Boston Way
Lanham, MD 20706

Manufactured in the United States of America

10 9 8 7 6 5 4 3 2 1

Books are available in quantity for promotional or premium use. Write to Director of Special Sales, Regnery Publishing, Inc., One Massachusetts Avenue, NW, Washington, DC 20001, for information on discounts and terms or call (202) 216-0600.

To my wife, Mona, and son, Tom, for their love and support. And to my brother Dick, killed in action in Vietnam; his son Michael, Silver Star, Afghanistan '03; and my brother Jim, Maj. General, USAF, (Ret.), who still holds the record for the most SAM-sites destroyed in history.

—TGM

To my wife, Muffin, my daughter, Dana, and my son, Scott.

—PEV

CONTENTS

ABOUT THE AUTHORS

LT. GEN. THOMAS MCINERNEY retired from the U.S. Air Force as assistant vice chief of staff of the Air Force and director for the Defense Performance Review. A respected military analyst, he appears regularly on the FOX News Channel, is a frequent nationally syndicated radio lecturer and guest, and has written for the *Wall Street Journal*, the *Washington Times*, the *Washington Post*, and *USA Today*. He is a graduate of the U.S. Military Academy and earned a master's degree in international relations from George Washington University.

MAJ. GEN. PAUL E. VALLELY retired from the U.S. Army as deputy commanding general, Pacific. He is the senior military analyst for the FOX News Channel, a regular guest lecturer and guest on nationally syndicated radio shows, and has served on numerous U.S. security assistance missions. He is a graduate of the U.S. Military Academy and served in many overseas theaters, as well as two combat tours in Vietnam.

PREFACE

THIS SECOND EDITION of *Endgame* goes to press as we mark the fifth anniversary of the beginning of the war on terror or, to be more precise, the war on radical Islam. We and our allies have had enormous successes: the liberation of Afghanistan, the liberation of Iraq, the capture of Saddam Hussein, new democratic governments established in Afghanistan and Iraq, and an improving situation in Lebanon. We have also had significant setbacks: the July 2005 terror bombings in London, the terror campaign against a democratic Iraq, and the deaths of U.S. and coalition military personnel.

Despite oceans of bad news funneled to us daily by the ill-informed and tendentious mainstream media, the fact is that we are winning the war. To say otherwise is to be hugely and deliberately dishonest. That dishonesty, rife in the liberal media, is having its effect on public opinion and is endangering our war effort, which depends on the determination of the American people to see us through to victory. The book presents a blueprint for victory, as relevant now as it was in 2004. Here we provide new information on how to meet the challenge of a nuclear Iran, and we have updated and revised the chapters to reflect reality in 2006.

As part of that revision, we think it is important to note here that there are thousands of documents from the Saddam Hussein regime that have still not been translated, and countless intelligence leads that have not been followed up but that might help explain the alleged mystery of Saddam Hussein's weapons of mass destruction (WMD) program and other aspects of the war on terror.

We got a taste of some likely revelations when in late February 2006 we attended the privately organized Intelligence Summit. This conference included a variety of experts, ranging from American defense and security analysts to retired British diplomat Julian Walker. Among the speakers was John Shaw, the former deputy undersecretary of defense for international technology security. He was the Pentagon official responsible for ensuring that "militarily critical technology" was not exported to suspect countries and companies. He has years of experience in the field of export control. Most important, he reaffirmed previous intelligence—which we reported in the first edition of this book—which indicated that immediately prior to the Iraqi campaign, Saddam Hussein hid his arsenal of WMD in Syria and Lebanon.

Shaw was officially tasked with documenting how Saddam Hussein accumulated his conventional weapons stockpile: an astounding 100 million tons of munitions. But as part of that work, he and his staff became involved in finding out what had happened to Iraq's WMD programs. Shaw detailed how, in his estimation, Saddam Hussein hid his WMD from the coalition.

Shaw's research included talking to Ukrainian and British intelligence officers and retired Lieutenant General James Clapper of the U.S. Air Force, the former head of the Defense Intelligence Agency.

Shaw discovered that Yevgeni Primakov—a Russian Middle East expert with KGB ties, who previously served as Russia's foreign minister and prime minister—went to Baghdad in December 2002. Primakov allegedly supervised Russian units in Iraq whose assignment was to cleanse the country of WMD and related documents, because they would have revealed Russian complicity with the regime. The units that carried out this "cleansing" were drawn from the GRU (Russian military intelligence) and Russian special operations forces, the renowned *Spetznaz*, and were commanded by two very senior retired Russian officers. These two officers, he was told, received decorations from the Iraqi government for their work in moving these weapons.

Attendees at the summit also heard recordings of Saddam Hussein and his henchmen discussing how they could hide WMD programs from United Nations inspectors—about whom they appeared to have insider information. They also specifically discussed a nuclear weapons program. These recordings were presented by John Tierney, a former translator with the FBI.

Most shocking was Saddam's prediction of a WMD attack against the United States that, he said, will not be blamed on Iraq. The exact meaning of the discussion is ambiguous, but we believe that Saddam meant that Iraq would mount such attacks through a proxy. In fact, we think that there is a very good chance that the anthrax attacks that took place in the United States in November 2001 were executed on the orders of Saddam Hussein.

The revelations of these tapes and this testimony remain controversial. So too is the administration's failure to translate the reams of captured Iraqi documents. There seems to be scant interest in investigating these documents and continuing the search for Iraqi WMD—and we think we know why.

While digging through these Iraqi files, investigators are bound to find irrefutable and embarrassing evidence of how much support various countries gave to Saddam Hussein before the war. Shaw says that the top three suppliers of conventional arms to Iraq—arms that are now in the hands of the Saddamite dead-enders and jihadists killing Iraqis and coalition troops—were Russia, France, and China. All three of these countries sit on the United Nations Security Council. With a confrontation with Iran becoming a certainty, the Bush administration will not want to alienate these countries; they could be enormously helpful in building a diplomatic, even military, coalition against Iran—a coalition that must be assembled as quickly as possible.

In *Endgame*, we focus on military strategy and military solutions. But we don't ignore the need for a political strategy, an economic strategy, and even a cultural strategy.

During the Cold War, the United States and its allies supported a wide variety of cultural exchanges and broadcast outlets like the Voice of America, Radio Free Europe, and Radio Liberty to present our ideals of freedom to the Communist world.

Today we need a cultural strategy to counter al-Qaeda and other radical Islamist groups. They present themselves as the vanguard of a global Islamist empire that will restore the glories of the ancient Baghdad-based caliphate. The reality, of course, is that they would like to turn the world into what Afghanistan was during the Taliban regime: a totalitarian Islamist state, where such "crimes" as keeping a song bird or watching a video result in savage beatings, where men who do not grow beards are thrown in jail, where women are banned from receiving an education or from working, where children are forbidden to fly kites, and where cultural artifacts or works of art that are not Islamic are destroyed. Too many in the Muslim world find this vision attractive. They consider the West a foe of Islam, they believe the West deliberately poisons the Islamic world with a decadent culture, and they are happy to applaud a group like al-Qaeda that attacks us.

At the 2006 Intelligence Summit, we encountered two extraordinary men: Walid Shoebat, formerly of the Palestinian Liberation Organization, and Dr. Tawfik Hamid, a former member of the Egyptian Islamist group Jamaat al-Islamiyya. Both men now reject terrorism and extremism. They do not reject Islam, but they do reject Wahhabi Islam, the puritanical sect that is the official religion of Saudi Arabia, and which the oil-rich Saudis bankroll around the world with billions of dollars a year, funding Wahhabi schools, universities, and mosques. The message of Wahhabi Islam, according to Shoebat and Hamid, meshes perfectly with the message of al-Qaeda and other radical groups.

The attraction of Islamic radicalism, however, obviously goes deeper. The Islamist violence spans the globe, from Kashmir to

France, from the Philippines to the Netherlands, from Nigeria to Indonesia, from Chechnya to Australia. The cultural challenge for United States and the West is thus enormous: It is no less than marginalizing the extremist branches of Islam—or at least blunting their appeal. It means presenting the West as the friend of Muslims who desire freedom and peace and tolerance, and presenting radical Islamists as our common enemy.

However, we need to be realistic. The future of Islam lies in the hands of the Muslims themselves. It is not for us to secularize their societies or tell them the proper interpretation of the Koran. What we can do is stand with moderate Muslims—and moderate Muslim regimes—against the radicals. We can provide a platform for moderate Islam through our own broadcast channels; we can address the Muslim world directly through satellite TV receivers; and we can present our own case for the virtues of peace, freedom, and the rule of law. We in the West would win ourselves more friends in the Islamic world if we presented a better public face. Pervasive pornography, coarse television programs, the leftist culture of Western self-hatred are no more attractive to Muslims than they are to our own better sense of ourselves. We need to do a better job broadcasting who we really are to the Islamic world.

We discuss these issues in greater detail in the pages that follow. Suffice it to say that a cultural campaign is necessary, but we know all too well that "soft power" is not sufficient. We are at war, and, as in all wars, strong diplomacy, decisive military action, and resolute leadership will ultimately determine the outcome.

We wrote this book to show the American people how this war against radical Islamism can and must be won—how we can swiftly move to the endgame of victory.

PART ONE

THE FIGHT WE'RE IN

CHAPTER ONE

GETTING TO THE ENDGAME

TODAY, AMERICA IS AT WAR with an enemy every bit as dangerous as Nazi Germany or the Soviet Union: We know it as radical Islam. Like enemies of our past, it draws upon the enforcement of a total ideology that rejects all that is "decadent" about Western liberal democracy. Memories of past glories and promises of their restoration as part of a new golden age fuel this movement that demands unflinching loyalty and ruthlessly stamps out all opposition. It excuses mass murder as necessary and extols the murderers. But it only takes a little investigation to reveal that its promises of liberation are a dubious cover for the blood-spattered tyranny that lies beneath.

If radical Islam were confined to a few benighted countries, we could merely denounce its brutality and celebrate when it was reformed, from afar. Radical Islamists, however, have global ambitions. They are not—and will never be—content with remaking Muslim countries along the totalitarian lines of Talibanic Afghanistan. Instead, they want to bring this totalitarian theocracy, founded on a muddled, bastardized notion of a bygone "Golden Age," to the entire world. They see the West as the implacable enemy of Islam, and Western culture and political ideas as the West's prime weapons against Islam. Radical Islamists view the war against the West as an extension of the one waged against Islamic expansionism from the *Reconquista* in Spain and the Crusades to the

battles of Malta, Lepanto, Vienna, and Budapest. To achieve final victory against the West and its allies around the world, radical Islamists
have founded a loose confederation of nation-states, terrorist groups,
and supporters of all stripes that we call the Web of Terror. Using countries such as Iran and Afghanistan as bases (and even some areas of
countries allied in the war on terror like Pakistan and the Philippines),
terrorist organizations such as al-Qaeda, Hezbollah, Palestinian Islamic
Jihad, Hamas, Jemaah Islamiah, and Abu Sayyaf have committed atrocities around the globe to advance the cause of radical Islam. Drawing on
the oil wealth of Saudi Arabia, radical clerics have established mosques
and religious schools around the world that spread a militant, inflexible, and intolerant version of Islam, serve as centers of recruitment for
terrorist organizations, and raise financial support for those organizations. The Web of Terror's number-one enemy—and thus its number-
one target—is the United States, because without the sword and shield
provided by the U.S. military, the rest of the West will have no choice
but to submit.

It has been widely reported that Osama bin Laden saw America's
tepid reaction to terrorist acts against it in the 1980s and the 1990s as
proof that the United States no longer had the will to protect itself. He
reasoned that one spectacular blow at the symbols of American power
would be enough to bring our country to its knees and make the world
capitulate to his dreams of a new Islamic empire. Fortunately, the
Bush administration was different from the Clinton administration; it
accepted that the United States was in a war and did not try to minimize the terrorist acts as a law enforcement problem. Because President Bush decided to deal with the Web of Terror forthrightly and was
unafraid to use American power—in its many forms—within two
years of the attacks of September 11, 2001, the United States and its
allies have overthrown two of the most important regimes within the
Web of Terror.

But the war is not over. The prospect of a free and democratic Iraq
and Afghanistan is threatened by the Islamists who would return

these countries to tyranny. Syria's army and intelligence services openly help terrorists, weapons, and money flow into Iraq and act as a conduit for Iranian cadres, materiel, and money to enter Lebanon, the Gaza Strip, and the West Bank. The Iranian regime is training and supporting terrorists, including those attacking our soldiers in Iraq, and is working feverishly to develop nuclear weapons. Iran's efforts to develop nuclear weapons has been advanced by Pakistani nuclear scientists and Saudi Arabian petro-dollars as well as support from the ultimate rogue state, North Korea. Unless the West takes determined and concerted action against the ever more assertive and combative Iranian regime, we have no doubt that Iran's quest for nuclear weapons will bear fruit in the very near future.

In North Korea, the dictator Kim Jong Il has impoverished his country and starved his people in order to build nuclear weapons and guided missiles—technologies he will certainly sell to radical Muslims with whom he has made common cause.

Post–September 11, the members of the Web of Terror have realized that America is more resilient than they thought. Therefore, its plans have grown more dramatic. We fear—and that is the correct word—that the next major terrorist attack on the United States will be conducted with weapons of mass destruction, particularly nuclear weapons. That is why we must act now to destroy the terror masters before they can strike us.

Our book is meant to provide a blueprint for victory, an endgame that will eliminate the Web of Terror. We speak not as armchair generals, but as retired generals of the Air Force and the Army who have devoted the bulk of our lives to defending the United States. We speak also as military analysts for FOX News Channel, positions that have allowed us to keep up-to-the-minute with all that is occurring in the Pentagon, the CIA, and elsewhere in the U.S. government related to the war on terrorism.

We also know the men and women on "the sharp edge" of the war on terror, in the rifle companies, artillery batteries, tank platoons,

Special Operating Forces, bomber wings, airlift squadrons, communications detachments, fighter squadrons, aircraft carriers, submarines, cruisers, destroyers, and amphibious warfare ships. These are the people who do the fighting, the "nation-building" and, inevitably, the dying. During our visits to Iraq over the past few years—including ones we made in late 2005—these dedicated Americans were uniform in the opinion that the war on terror was worth fighting; that we are winning, slowly but surely, in Iraq; and that the only threat to the progress we have made against the Web of Terror is the lack of will on the part of the American people. In short, they understand why we fight—and they want their fellow citizens to understand it too.

Lt. General Tom McInerney writes as an expert on high-tech warfare who served for thirty-five years in the U.S. Air Force. Tom was a career fighter pilot who served four tours in Vietnam, commanded a numbered air force during a major strike against a terrorist country, and was a joint force commander (his command was composed of the 6th Infantry Division [Light] and the 11th Air Force and was supported by the Navy's Third Fleet). His final assignment was as the assistant vice chief of staff of the U.S. Air Force and director of the Defense Performance Review, reporting directly to the secretary of defense. Maj. General Paul Vallely writes as an expert on special operations, psychological/information warfare, and civil-military operations. Like Tom, he is a graduate of West Point. In fact, we were at West Point together—Tom started life as an infantry officer before transferring to the Air Force—but we never crossed paths again, despite serving in Vietnam at the same time, until FOX News Channel brought us together as military analysts after September 11. Paul served in the Army for thirty-two years, seeing two combat tours in Vietnam and duty around the world before retiring as deputy commanding general, U.S. Army, Pacific. As military analysts at FOX News Channel, we developed the network's "war room." More important, we were recognized as the military analysts who got things right more often than anyone else in the popular media. In part that was because of our sources, and in part it was because we based our analysis on fact, not spin, and what we knew of the United States military's capabilities, not on the hopes or fears or on what other commentators were saying. In this book, our intention is to offer the same kind of analysis—factual, doable, realistic.

KNOW YOUR ENEMY

The first step in confronting our enemy is to know it, define it, and deal with it. The Web of Terror is made up of eight terror-sponsoring countries. The qualifications to be a Web of Terror nation are that it supports and/or sponsors terrorism and is involved with weapons of mass destruction. Without the support of these countries, terrorist groups like al-Qaeda would not be a serious threat. Our mission is to defeat al-Qaeda by defeating the Web of Terror. In other words, they have a choice to take a path of cooperation or a path of defiance. That means changing, or achieving major policy shifts in, six of the regimes that make up the Web of Terror, and helping guide the other two on a path of political reform. The six are Afghanistan, Iraq, Iran, Syria, North Korea, and Libya. Of these six regimes, the United States has forcibly changed two already. Afghanistan was the nest of the Taliban and al-Qaeda. It no longer is. Saddam Hussein's Iraq was in many ways the center of gravity of the Web of Terror. It was central geographically, bordering Syria, Iran, and Saudi Arabia. It was central in its contempt for the West with its daily violations of UN resolutions, firing on British and American aircraft, and continuation of WMD research and development. It was central in that it had produced and used WMD in the past. And it was central because it was a way station for terrorists who could contact scientists working on WMD research, something that America's former weapons inspector David Kay not only affirmed but said was more likely than we ever realized. The Hussein regime had already once tried to assassinate a former American president—George H. W. Bush. Certainly, it would have had

few compunctions about giving ricin, anthrax, or some other poisonous agent to a terrorist group for a strike against the United States, if
Iraq could maintain plausible deniability.

Of the remaining regimes:

Libya still shows signs of trying to differentiate itself from other
members of the Web of Terror. Based on his long and sorry track
record of supporting and committing terrorism, the dictator of this
country, Muammar Gaddafi, cannot ever be considered our ally or
completely trusted. However, he has taken the cue from the disposal
of Saddam Hussein's regime and abandoned his quest for nuclear
weapons and, insofar as we can tell, his active support of terrorism.

Syria continues to be a major sponsor of terrorism. Immediately
after the liberation of Iraq, it made noises about reaching some form
of accommodation with Israel. The trouble is that, at the same time, it
granted refuge to the remnants of Saddam Hussein's intelligence services, army, and paramilitary forces. These forces almost immediately
began to work with Ba'athist loyalists within Iraq and Islamists aching
for a chance to kill Americans to conduct the terrorist campaign that
has plagued Iraq for years. For too long, terrorists—including suicide
bombers—passed over Syria's border with Iraq freely, fueling the campaign of murder that has taken the lives of thousands of people.

2005, however, was a bad year for Syria. In February, a huge bomb
killed former Lebanese prime minister Rafik Hariri and many others
in Beirut. Hariri's open hostility to Syria's continued occupation of
Lebanon, manipulation of its government and politics, and exploita-
tion of its economy since 1990 made Syria the obvious culprit in his
death. In the resulting "Cedar Revolution," a series of massive public
demonstrations brought together nearly every faction of Lebanon's
often fractious society—Druze, Sunni, and Christian—in pursuit of
one goal: ending Syria's presence in and influence over Lebanon. Sul-
lenly, Syria withdrew its army and intelligence agents (at least some

of them) and new elections in the withdrawal's wake led to a robust anti-Syrian presence in Lebanon's parliament. However, the assassination of Gibran Tueni, a prominent Lebanese journalist known for frank criticism of Syria's policies toward Lebanon—including its corruption of Lebanon's political system and government—and for running a newspaper that often published articles by Syrian dissidents in late 2005, demonstrated that Syria remains intent on exercising some control over events in Lebanon.

In December 2005, the authoritative *Jane's Defense Weekly* reported that, in the previous month, Syria had signed an agreement with Iran, its longtime ally and its most generous sponsor since the fall of the Soviet Union. The agreement states that Syria will store Iranian nuclear weapons and materials on its territory should the United Nations impose sanctions on Iran. Syria also agreed to continue supporting—by means of weapons, munitions, and other support—the Lebanon-based Hezbollah. For its part, Iran agreed to provide safe haven for Syrian intelligence officers indicted by Lebanon or the United Nations as well as to help Syria improve its weapons. Such weapons include chemical weapons and ballistic missiles, "advanced weapon systems" in the event of a military "confrontation."

Nevertheless, for all the trouble it causes and all the murder it supports in the region, the Syrian regime is a paper tiger that could crumple if enough pressure is applied to it.

Iran is a great danger because of its rush to build a nuclear weapon and because it is the heart of the Web of Terror. President Jimmy Carter's decision to let the Shah of Iran fall was a monumental one. In a sense, the Ayatollah Khomeini was the spider that spun the Web of Terror. Iran, until 1979, had been a moderately Western-oriented country and an ally to the United States. After the revolution of 1978–1979, it became the nation where a revolutionary Islamic fundamentalist state was first established. As such it provided other radical Islamists with an encouraging example that even the most apparently resilient regime could be overthrown by a dedicated cadre of activists and that a forthrightly Islamic regime could be established in its stead and enjoy broad popular support (for a time, at least). Under the control of those who toppled the Shah, Iran also became a leading exporter of radical Islam and a leading supporter of Islamist terrorism. Some analysts also have stated that the rise of a Shi'ite Islamic state in Iran spurred the House of Saud to expand its efforts to spread its ascetic Wahabbi theology, which has spawned a large number of problems. Now, however, the open and growing domestic opposition to Iran's despotic mullahs is bringing the political situation in Iran to the point where regime change might be easier to accomplish in Iran than it was in Iraq.

The last country is the Web of Terror's one non-Islamic component, North Korea. Too many policymakers take the position that there is very little we can do to reform North Korea, because we can bring no viable military pressure to bear on it, given North Korea's fanatically militarized regime. That argument is false, and later in the book we will show why.

There are two regimes that need reforming: one is Saudi Arabia, whose enormous standing and financial resources in the Islamic world have been used to promote the Web of Terror—often in ways contrary to the kingdom's own interests. The other regime is Pakistan, which has an unfortunate record of advancing radical Islamist groups through official and quasi-official means. Pakistan's current president, General Pervez Musharraf, has shown great bravery and no little nerve in confronting his country's rogue nuclear scientists and trying to tame the Islamists in Pakistan's political and military establishments. However, the situation in Pakistan is not as much improved as we hoped it would be when we wrote the first edition of this book.

Change the regimes in these countries, or reform them, and the Web of Terror withers away—and that includes al-Qaeda and the "subsidiaries" in its terror conglomerate. Countering al-Qaeda's terrorism as a police matter will not end it. Focusing solely on al-Qaeda's amorphous network and not on the rogue states that give it sustenance will not destroy it. The Web of Terror nurtured and supported al-Qaeda and its related organizations. Destroy the Web of Terror and al-Qaeda is destroyed and with it, the chief threat to America's security today: weapons of mass destruction in the hands of terrorists.

Any other solution is incomplete—and, by being incomplete, dangerous. The scenarios if we don't act are frightening, which only underlines why they must be avoided. It's time to consider them now.

CHAPTER TWO

THE NIGHTMARES

O UR ENEMY, THE RADICAL Islamists, dream of resurrecting the great Muslim empire that once spanned the Middle East, North Africa, the Balkans, and parts of Central Asia, and of establishing an Islamic super-state that stretches from Malaysia's border with Thailand through Indonesia, the largest Muslim country in the world, to the southern Philippines. They even foresee an Islamic conquest of Europe, through the influence of radical mullahs in European mosques, through the infiltration of radical Islamist terrorist cells into Western countries, and through the demographic growth of Islamic populations versus the declining populations of secular or Christian Europe. Their dream is to create a global empire with the likes of Osama bin Laden or the Taliban's former leader Mullah Omar at its head. The Islamists' dream is the West's nightmare.

But even if the radical Islamists' dream is overblown, they and their Stalinist cohort, North Korea, could nevertheless present the United States with several nightmare scenarios. Here they are, in rising levels of importance.

THE LEBANONIZATION OF IRAQ

Until the late 1960s, Israel's and Syria's neighbor, Lebanon, though never entirely free from strife, was known for its relative stability, peace, and prosperity. Set on the Mediterranean Sea, its capital Beirut was a great trading city—and European holiday destination—renowned for its beauty and sophistication. All that changed after Lebanon was caught literally in the crossfire of the Arab-Israeli dispute, which caused Lebanon's own religious divisions to boil over into civil war and chaos.

Today, although Syria has pulled its army and intelligence services out of Lebanon, the assassinations of 2005 evidence a continued presence and influence, albeit a shadowy one, in that country. Lebanon's emergence from Syrian control and influence will be relatively slow and will be complicated by the fact that southern Lebanon is dominated by the Iranian-sponsored and supported terrorist group, Hezbollah, the yellow flag of which we have seen defiantly flying when we visited the Israel–Lebanon border near Metulla.

Turning Iraq, with its rich oil and gas fields, into another Lebanon— that is, a state where a foreign power dominates the country and turns it to terrorist ends—is a major goal of the Web of Terror and especially of the Iranian government.

Iraq's strategic position is crucial to the Middle East, with a port on the Persian Gulf, and borders with Iran, Turkey, Syria, Kuwait, and Jordan. Allow Iraq to develop a democratic state and political culture, and you have a friendly neighbor to such moderate, pro-Western countries as Kuwait, Turkey, and Jordan—as well as a much more hopeful future for the region. Let it fall prey to Iran's mullahs, Ba'athist "deadenders," and radical Islamists, and you have a fragmented country torn apart by sectarian strife and a new base for radical Islamist terror and subversion—sitting on top of vast oil and gas reserves.

Lebanon was home to many different ethnic and religious groups— Sunni, Shi'ite, Maronite Christian (many of whom were driven out of the country), and Druze. Iraq, too, is home to many different ethnic and religious groups—Sunni, Shi'ite, Kurds, Turkmen, and a small but historic minority of Christians. As Lebanon was largely a creation of the French Republic after World War I, Iraq was a creation of the British Empire. Now, the glue that held the country together since

1958, the national socialist Ba'ath Party, which adhered to the 1950s-vintage ideology of "Arab nationalism" is gone. With the roots of democratic governance still not deeply set, the likes of Iran and Syria would like nothing better than to tear Iraq apart and grab some of the pieces for themselves. That's what makes the presence of U.S. and coalition troops so vital in Iraq. If we continue to help Iraq develop into a stable, democratic state, it will mark a major advance against the Web of Terror.

          I   I   I   I   I   I   I   I   I

We know that Iran is hard at work trying to undermine Iraq and has been since the summer of 2003. Agents of Iran's ministry of intelligence and security and cadres of Iran's Revolutionary Guard Corps infiltrated Shi'ite-dominated areas of Iran and brought in weapons, money, and materiel. The Shi'ite political organization, the Supreme Council for the Islamic Revolution in Iran (SCIRI), a longtime opponent of Saddam Hussein's regime, is widely considered one of Iran's political proxies in Iraq. Its armed force, the Badr Brigade, is essentially an Iranian-backed militia. If the Iranian regime becomes more assertive, it might prod the Badr Brigade to take on Iraqi security services directly in a bid to disrupt and dismember Iraq.

The Mahdi Army, the militia of radical Shi'ite cleric Muqtada al-Sadr, is strong in some Shi'ite areas in Iraq as well as in the Shi'ite neighborhoods of Baghdad. In the summer of 2004, this force took on U.S. forces in the city of Najaf in a stand-up fight. Predictably, the U.S. Marines defeated the Mahdi Army; however, many of its fighters fled into a famous mosque in Najaf, and it took the intervention of SCIRI's chief, Grand Ayatollah Ali al-Sistani, to prevent them from making a stand and forcing the Marines to assault them in the mosque.

Although this incident occurred more than eighteen months ago, it still concerns us because Iran's leaders have become even more intransigent in terms of foreign policy and even more heated in their rhetoric, drawing on an apocalyptic vision of the future of Islam. The vast majority of Iraqis—including most Shi'ites—are content to take their chances within Iraq's democratic politics. The mullahs of Iran and their allies in the government, however, fired by this vision, are apparently ready to discount these desires in order to fulfill their own imperial designs in the region. If the Iranians devote themselves to disrupting political and civil life in Iraq—either by attempting to widen sectarian divisions politically or by undermining Iraqis' confidence in the nascent Iraqi state by terrorism—it might corrode any sense of national identity.

The only way the radical Islamists can influence the progress of Iraq are assassination, subversion, sabotage, propaganda, and terrorism. Their goal is obvious: to turn Iraq into another Lebanon.

CHANGE FOR THE DEVIL WE KNOW: THE HOUSE OF SAUD

Many people would not shed a tear if the House of Saud disappeared overnight. Taken as a whole, the behavior of the Saudi royal family can be maddening. Although its members are usually pro-American, it also provides sinecures and lucrative financial support to clerics and scholars who teach radical Islam and issue *fatwas* that give religious approval to the most heinous acts of terrorism in Saudi Arabia and throughout the world. At home, despite some recent changes, the House of Saud cannot be described as anything but a repressive regime. It is regarded as an ally of the United States—but conducts the alliance almost strictly on its own terms. Our concerns with the House of Saud, however, are tempered by the realization that whatever and whoever replaced its hundreds of princes could be much worse.

Until May 2003, the House of Saud's grip on its country looked firm. But an informed analyst will tell you that only one in four Saudi subjects—the technocrats, military officers, diplomats, and businessmen who have been educated in, or have extensive dealings with, the

West—is unflinchingly loyal to the House of Saud. The other three-quarters of the Saudi population view the ruling house and its denizens as hypocrites who fund mosques, religious schools, and Islamic universities and are the custodians of Islam's two holiest sites, Mecca and Medina. They see them as both corrupt—running the country exclusively in their own interest—and corrupted by the forbidden pleasures of the West.

Some, including many members of the royal family, argue that the House of Saud would gain popularity if it created a written, democratic constitution (it currently asserts that its constitution is the Koran) and held elections. On the other hand, many analysts predict that any democratic elections would make Osama bin Laden, or his equivalent, prime minister of Saudi Arabia.

While some constitutional reform is possible, the reality is that the House of Saud is in a showdown with the radical Islamists. In this fight, the House of Saud would seem to have the upper hand, with an extensive and effective internal security apparatus and control of the nation's religious establishment. Moreover, the House of Saud has not one but two guard units drawn from the Sauds' own tribe and separate from the army—the Royal Guard Battalion and the larger Saudi Arabian National Guard—that will loyally defend the regime.

While this offers some reassurance, the example of the Shah of Iran should be instructive to the Saudi royal family. The Shah had a large and dreaded secret police—SAVAK—and an Imperial Guard consisting of two well-equipped divisions. As impressive as they were, both the Shah's police apparatus and the Imperial Guard were not enough to overcome Iran's popular Islamist revolution. Reports that Islamists have penetrated the Saudi military and police as well as other government institutions now surface with disturbing regularity. All of this raises the nightmare scenario of the fall of Saudi Arabia and the establishment of the Islamic Republic of Arabia and of a state as radical as Afghanistan under the Taliban, but incomparably wealthier.

Consider what al-Qaeda was able to accomplish when it was headquartered in two wretchedly poor nations, Sudan and Afghanistan: the bombings of American embassies in Africa, the development of a worldwide terror network, the bombing of the USS *Cole*, and the attacks on September 11, 2001. Now think what a radical Islamist regime could do with full access to Saudi Arabia's petro-dollars and relatively well-developed infrastructure. Islamist terrorists from Indonesia, the Philippines, Nigeria, and elsewhere would travel to Saudi Arabia; meet with the heads of the Arabian Republic's intelligence and security services; and ask for money, weapons, manpower, training centers, and transport to attack Western interests and moderate Muslims. Remember how the damage to oil and gas facilities in the Gulf of Mexico caused by hurricanes in 2005 caused crude oil prices to spike to more than $60 a barrel and gasoline prices to jump to more than $3 a gallon. This gives us an idea of the economic consequences if crude oil prices increased to $100, $150, or more a barrel. An Islamist Republic of Arabia could cripple the economies of the United States, Europe, and even Japan simply by shutting off the flow of oil. In his book on U.S.-Saudi relations, *Sleeping with the Devil*, former CIA officer Robert Baer estimates that in such a scenario the price of oil could skyrocket to $150 a barrel. If the Arabian Republic were able to intimidate the ruling families of the relatively small Gulf States, the price could go even higher. Unlike the monarchs who rule Saudi Arabia and the Gulf States, Islamist revolutionaries believe in destroying the West, not necessarily trading with the West; they would have no compunction about devastating Western economies even at the cost of hundreds of billions of dollars in lost revenue. They also could use the oil weapon to divide the West by holding out the prospect of a renewed flow of oil in exchange for pro-Islamist policies of appeasement, effectively turning some Western governments, desperate to do just about anything to keep the oil flowing, into de facto allies against the United States and its partners.

NUCLEAR NIGHTMARE I: NORTH KOREA'S SUICIDE

In early October 2003, North Korea announced that, through the reprocessing of spent nuclear fuel rods, it had enough plutonium to begin
the production of nuclear weapons. Some dismiss this as typical
North Korean braggadocio or the opening move in an attempt to shake
down the Americans, Chinese, and Russians for the fuel, food, and
other support needed to prop up the North Korean regime. However,
based on the fact that North Korea has not only poured huge amounts
of money and manpower into developing nuclear weapons, but has
also assisted Iran's efforts to build nuclear weapons, we think that
these threats must be taken seriously.

| | | | | | | | | |

If North Korea builds and demonstrates nuclear weapons, Japan's
leaders will undoubtedly consider North Korea's previous ballistic
missile tests—and decide to develop their own nuclear capability.
Even South Korea could embark on a program to get its own
weapons—it has the technology, and much better financial resources
than North Korea.

But a "nuclearized" Northeast Asia is not our main concern. We
think that the North Korean regime considers nuclear weapons as the
key to its conquest of South Korea. It could brandish nuclear weapons
at Japan and the United States (the latter if it manages to complete the
development of long-range ICBMs), threatening to use them against
these countries if they dare come to South Korea's defense. Essentially,
the North Koreans would pose a question to the United States and
Japan: Respectively, are you willing to put Honolulu, Anchorage, and
Seattle and Tokyo, Kyoto, and Yokohama at risk of nuclear annihilation in order to defend Seoul and Pusan? North Korea thinks the
answer is no. We think the answer is yes. The real answer, however,
is to prevent North Korea from acquiring nuclear weapons in the first
place.

NUCLEAR NIGHTMARE II: IRAN

It is prudent to think that Iran's crash nuclear program will bear fruit in the form of an operational weapon at any moment, because whether Iran has weapons a month or a year after this book is published, we must consider what the Tehran regime will do with them. Judging from the rhetoric of Iran's new president (a former commander in Iran's Revolutionary Guard Corps and quite possibly a leader in the 1979 takeover of the U.S. embassy by Iranian "students"), which has included calls for the elimination of Israel, there is every reason to believe that Iran will use nuclear weapons to advance a bold strategic agenda. This agenda will affect not only Israel but also the rest of the Middle East and South Asia, including Afghanistan and Pakistan. This is not to say that Iran will *use* nuclear weapons against its enemies around the region. It can be counted upon, however, to use such weapons as a means of intimidation in an attempt to impose its will on its neighbors.

One likely scenario is that Iran would use its nuclear weapons or sale of a North Korean nuclear weapon to terrorists to "solve" the Palestinian question to its satisfaction. If brought together by their Iranian sponsors or placed under the "temporary" command of Iranian Revolutionary Guard cadres, Hamas and Palestinian Islamic Jihad would have two major advantages over the Palestinian Authority's competing military elements—unity of command and unity of purpose.

In early 2006, the corrupt and ineffectual al-Fatah, devoid of the unifying leadership of Yasser Arafat, was routed in parliamentary elections in Palestinian areas by the Iranian-backed Islamist terrorist organization Hamas. Hamas and its like-minded ally, Palestinian Islamic Jihad, almost certainly will exile and exterminate their political opponents and co-opt al-Fatah's more radical elements, such as the al-Aqsa Martyrs Brigade. Afterward, we expect that these two groups would mount a massive terror campaign against Israel from the West Bank and the Gaza Strip and that the other strong Iranian proxy based in southern Lebanon, Hezbollah, would strike northern Israel at the same time. Iran might declare that any Israeli counterstrikes into southern Lebanon, the West Bank, and the Gaza Strip would be met by a nuclear response. Israel would face the choice of a nuclear exchange with Iran or accommodation with an Islamist Palestine on Iran's terms. Given that Iran's terms probably would be ridiculously draconian—perhaps the elimination of Israel as a state—Israel and Iran could very well fight the first nuclear war in history.

NUCLEAR NIGHTMARE III: ANOTHER SEPTEMBER 11

Almost two years after the attacks of September 11, 2001, we learned that the initial plan was to use ten airliners—five on the East Coast, five on the West Coast—as flying bombs. The deaths of more than three thousand people in the Pentagon, the World Trade Center, and Pennsylvania notwithstanding, the terrorists did not manage to inflict much long-term damage through their September 11 attacks. Commerce, air travel, and the financial markets quickly resumed, the federal government was fully functional, and the United States did not abandon its allies in the Middle East. We can only suppose, therefore, that if terrorists were to strike us again they would want to strike a truly devastating blow.

Our nightmare—made more nightmarish because it is so plausible—is that the next strike would consist of the simultaneous detonation of multiple nuclear weapons in many major cities in the United States such as New York, Washington, Detroit, Seattle, Los Angeles, Chicago, Atlanta, Houston, New Orleans, and Miami.

Getting the bombs or the components for the bombs into the United States would be simple. They are relatively small and easily concealed in larger cargo or in a shipping container. Smuggling them into the United States would not be difficult because, despite the steps taken after September 11, 2001, our borders remain inexcusably porous. If the price was right, the criminal gangs that currently move illegal narcotics and immigrants into this country would help smuggle nuclear weapons and/or nuclear materials over our borders. The bombs would not have to be huge "city busters." Weapons with even the relatively small yield of twenty kilotons and exploded on the ground (nuclear weapons exploded in the air are more destructive) would produce catastrophic results in the target cities.

Hundreds of thousands of Americans would be killed immediately; many more would be horridly wounded, a large number, mortally. Millions more would be consigned to a lifetime of worry about the effects of radiation poisoning on them and their families. Beyond the appalling human cost, there would be grave damage to the country's ability to govern itself, to function as a coherent economic unit, to communicate internally, to rebuild our cities, to aid our allies, and to strike back at our enemies. If the bomb meant for Washington were set off in front of the Library of Congress, it would destroy the Capitol and the Supreme Court, pulverize many government offices, including the Department of Health and Human Services (which has many crucial emergency functions), and kill thousands of people vital to the proper functioning of government—cabinet secretaries, civil servants, senators, and congressmen. If they survived the attack, the president, the vice president, and their staffs would move to a safe location, as would the surviving officials of any government departments fortunate enough to have headquarters a safe distance from Ground Zero. At once, the country's capital would be heavily damaged and largely abandoned by the government.

A bomb in midtown Manhattan would effectively wipe out important financial, corporate, and cultural institutions as well as destroy the headquarters of many of America's news media outlets and punch a mammoth hole in the heart of America's greatest city. The cities of Los Angeles and Miami are economic and financial gateways to the Pacific Rim and Latin America, respectively. Attacks on these cities, therefore, would not only damage the American economy but also have ripple effects far beyond the borders of the United States.

Of course, economic recovery would be the farthest thing from the minds of most Americans who would be dealing with the immediate effects of the attacks. Even in those cities not directly affected by the attacks, there probably would be damage to and disruption of electrical power, transportation, and communications systems. Unless it was immediately known that some form of federal executive authority was still in place—albeit not in Washington—there would be concerns about authority and coordination of recovery, military response, and security efforts. There might not be much, if any, knowledge of the true nature of the attack and its scope for days, maybe even weeks.

Once Americans understood *what* had happened, we still would not know exactly *how* it happened or *who* conducted the strike. Unlike the investigators of the Oklahoma City bombing, investigators would not find pieces of trucks that they could trace to rental agencies and to the bombers. Evidence would vaporize as part of the ultimate suicide bombing. Even more important, there would be a gnawing fear: Are there more weapons out there? Could there be other attacks on other American cities? Could other terror cells strike the cities already attacked?

If, after some time, we discovered that, say, al-Qaeda was the culprit, what would our reaction be? Would we invade the country where the terrorists have their headquarters? What if the headquarters are in Riyadh, Jakarta, or Islamabad? Would we issue a request for extradition? If intelligence revealed that Iran had a hand in the strike, how would we respond? Would we stay our hand from an all-out retaliation out of concern for the millions of truly innocent Iranians behind whom their government would be hiding?

No matter how we decided to respond, there is no guarantee that our allies would support us in that response. Knowing that nuclear weapons could be in their major cities, they could declare themselves neutral and deny us any support, material or otherwise. If those who attacked us seized that moment to attack Israel, the Europeans might

turn a blind eye to the situation and a deaf ear to pleas for help from
Jerusalem. Whatever else you might say about the Israelis, when it
comes to survival, they do not shrink from the task. Israel could
decide to mount a preemptive strike against Iran.

Many of the scenarios about terrorism concern "weapons of mass
destruction," otherwise known as nuclear, chemical, and biological
weapons. There is ample reason to believe that these weapons are in
the arsenals of some Web of Terror nations or soon will be. Knowing
these weapons' terrible effects, we should be deeply concerned about
the threat they pose to this country and our allies. As grave as the
threats posed by biological and chemical weapons are, however, they
are not as grave as that posed by nuclear weapons. As preparations for
dealing with the possibility of an influenza pandemic demonstrate,
steps to arrest or at least retard the spread of the disease can be taken.
We are relatively well prepared against biological attacks, and their
impact would likely be limited. A biological attack would not destroy
the infrastructure that our country depends on. Telephone lines would
be working. Electricity would be generated and transmitted. Highways
and railroads would remain open. Computer networks would remain
functioning. However frightening a biological attack might be in theory, it is unlikely to achieve much in fact.

Both of us served in Germany during the Cold War, and the threat
from the massive Soviet chemical arsenal was never far from our
minds—and with good reason. Chemical weapons' effects are grue-
some and, depending on the particular agent, the dose needed to kill
or severely injure can be small. Nevertheless, delivering these
weapons in a manner and quantity that would be sure to cause massive casualties would be no easy matter. These weapons are just as
deadly to the attacker as to the target and so demand careful handling.
Even if a terrorist group were given chemical weapons from the arsenal of a country, there is no guarantee that they would be able to transport them safely to the target cities or gather them in sufficient
quantities to kill and injure large numbers of people.

Most chemical weapons lose their effectiveness over time as wind, sun, and rain dissipate and dilute them. Moreover, there are proven, effective means to counter these weapons, contain their effects, and prevent casualties from mounting. And chemical weapons, like biological weapons, do not destroy buildings or bridges or any other vital infrastructure or interfere seriously in the operation of government.

From a military perspective, therefore, using nuclear weapons just makes more sense. Mounting a terrorist operation using weapons of mass destruction would be expensive, even if the most expensive item—the weapons themselves—were "donated" by Iran or North Korea. It would be extremely wasteful for the Web of Terror to expend immense amounts of time, money, and manpower on an operation that would *not* deliver a crushing blow to the United States.

Given the current crash weapons programs of Iran and North Korea and the questionable security of weapons under the control of Pakistan and Russia, a terrorist nuclear strike against the United States is more than possible. It is very likely. Preventing such an attack by arresting the proliferation of nuclear weapons among the members of the Web of Terror, therefore, must be of paramount concern for America's president.

NUCLEAR NIGHTMARE IV: REVENGE

In the immediate aftermath of the September 11 attacks, there was concern that the United States would retaliate in a way that one person described as "Going Roman"—the utter destruction of the sponsors of the terrorists who killed thousands of our citizens. Would the United States do to, say, Afghanistan what Rome did to Carthage? As events proved, the United States is not cast in the Roman mold; President Bush did not take the approach that characterizes so much of human history and launch a campaign of extermination in Afghanistan. Our campaign against the Taliban and al-Qaeda was a model of restraint. It would have been a far simpler matter to attack

Kabul and Kandahar from the air in hopes of pummeling the Taliban into submission and smashing al-Qaeda into atoms—as the U.S. Air Force's circling B-52s were quite capable of doing. Instead of destroying entire villages or large patches of Kabul, however, our commanders used our air power with more care and precision than in any previous war. Certainly, a country bent on exacting revenge and sowing fear would not have bothered to try to avoid hitting mosques, schools, and hospitals, as we did.

In Iraq, the fear of many—and apparent desire of some—was that Baghdad would be reduced to rubble, with American artillery and air power pulverizing the city, block by block. If that had been done, thousands of civilians would have been killed and wounded and many thousands more would have been made homeless. In stark contrast to the fears and dreams of some, the cities, towns, and villages of Iraq were left essentially intact, and far fewer Iraqis were killed or injured in the weeks of fighting in Operation Iraqi Freedom than the critics of the campaign had predicted with such utter certainty. It is important to note as well that the stated mission of the Iraqi campaign was not the subjugation of the Iraqi people, the destruction of Iraq's national identity, or the eradication of Iraqi culture. Quite the contrary, the campaign was about ousting a dictator who sponsored terrorism, pursued (and had used in the past) weapons of mass destruction, enslaved the Iraqi people, and bent Iraq's national identity and culture to his own ends. But if nuclear weapons are exploded on American soil, such carefully measured responses would not do. In response, the American president would indeed "go Roman." The instruments of counterstrike are on the tips of missiles in silos and on board submarines, ready for immediate launch. In the absence of absolute evidence pinpointing the source of such nuclear terror—and given that the Web of Terror is international in scope—the American government would still know that the nuclear bombs used could have come from only a limited number of countries. The most likely suspects would be Pakistan, Iran, and North Korea. And the money to fund such a bold operation would have come from a limited list of donors—most probably, Iran or Saudi Arabia. Teasing out the details of the plot would be left for later. International and domestic calls for restraint and warnings about "the Arab Street" would be irrelevant. Nuclear retaliation against Tehran, Pyongyang, and the capital of any other suspected regime would be a given.

If you don't think this scenario is likely then you have a higher opinion of human nature than we do. With many of our major cities shattered and millions of Americans dead or dying, an American president who did not retaliate in kind would not long remain president. The repercussions of American retaliation would be profound: the deaths of perhaps tens of millions, the shock and distrust of our allies, and a dividing line in domestic politics as stark as that of the Civil War.

We present this scenario as a warning of the consequences of inaction and appeasement against the Web of Terror. If we act now, revenge will not be necessary, because we can destroy the Web of Terror using less destructive strategies and tactics, such as we will outline in this book. The alternative is to sit back, trust in the good intentions of those regimes whose stated goal is our destruction, and be left with revenge as our only option.

We present this scenario of massive retaliation by the United States for another reason. Our enemies, and any supposed ally who would betray us, should know the risks they run. Critics might call it "cowboy justice." They might call it "international vigilantism." They might even call it "mass murder." But it is what would happen. Whoever attacked the United States in such a manner or assisted in any such attack against the United States would be utterly destroyed, their countries made radioactive wastelands. Our country could retaliate without breaking a sweat. One Trident missile submarine could do the job in sixty minutes, tops. Do we take a perverse pleasure in the prospect of so massive an American response? Far from it. As men who know what these weapons mean, this is a nightmare we want to avoid; avoiding it is a reason we wrote this book.

Some have said that the war on terror could last twenty-five, fifty, a hundred years. We cannot wait that long. We need to defeat the Web of Terror now, not just deter it for some indefinite period, hoping it runs out of gas or that time will somehow heal the perceived wounds that drive those who want us destroyed. State sponsors of terrorism must destroy the monsters they have created—or they themselves will be destroyed. Saudi Arabia and Pakistan must clean their own nests, while Iran, North Korea, Syria, and Libya either must change regimes, or, as Libya has professed to do, cease supporting terror and surrender any ambitions to develop weapons of mass destruction. As we will show, we can make that choice even simpler for them.

PART TWO

HOW WE FIGHT

CHAPTER THREE

NEW CAMPAIGNS, NEW STRATEGIES

OUR GRAND STRATEGIC GOAL is quite simple: to ensure the security of the United States by thoroughly defeating the Web of Terror. That means drying up the sources of weapons, funding, and manpower for terrorist groups, and denying them territorial sanctuaries. It means stopping nuclear proliferation and dismantling the WMD development programs and weapons stockpiles of rogue states. It means encouraging the spread of democracy in the Muslim world. And it means resolving the Palestinian question in a fair and equitable manner between two democratic entities—the State of Israel and a *reformed* Palestinian Authority.

We cannot wait to achieve these goals or expect that these changes will happen of their own volition. In some cases, achieving these goals will mean overthrowing regimes, as we did with the Taliban and Saddam Hussein, though the means by which we do so might vary. A case in point could be Iran. Even if Iran officially ends its nuclear weapons development program, it is doubtful that the Islamist hardliners who run the country will cease arming, training, and funding terror groups around the world. The only serious question remaining, therefore, is how to achieve regime change in Iran, and whether that will be done through support for the domestic resistance, diplomatic pressure, military force, or some combination of the three. In other

cases, we will have to engage in *regime preservation*, helping governments secure themselves against Islamist violence so that eventual
democratic reform is possible. Nuclear-armed Pakistan, for example,
could fall to an Islamist military coup or become a bloody battle-
ground between religious sects, secularists, and foreign jihadists. Pakistan's government, for the long-term benefit of all (except the
jihadists), needs democratic reform, but not before it neutralizes the
domestic Islamist threat.

The first key concept is the need to press at utmost speed the war
on terror to achieve regime change throughout the Web of Terror–
supporting states. Another key concept is preemption. President Bush
was right to make this a strategic principle of his administration. Preemption's purpose is to put teeth behind the idea that certain actions
are utterly unacceptable. Thumb your nose at UN weapons inspectors,
and the United States will not risk that it can trust you; it will, in fact,
enforce UN threats that the UN itself won't enforce. Sell or transfer
nuclear weapons and their delivery systems—cruise missiles and
ICBMs—to rogue states or terrorist groups, and America will stop you,
by force if necessary. It would be folly to let inaction lead to nuclear
proliferation, to wait until a nuclear weapon falls into the hands of al-
Qaeda or detonates in New York or London, before we act in our own
defense.

Another key concept is simultaneity. We simply do not have the
time to take a sequential approach: first Afghanistan, then Iraq, perhaps
next Iran, then maybe North Korea, and so on. Every strand in the Web
of Terror needs to be snipped—now. Thankfully, work *is* being done on
many fronts. However, it is not enough and it is not being done anywhere near fast enough. What follows next are the campaigns that must
be won.

Afghanistan

The key to lasting success in Afghanistan can be summed up in one
word: security. The opening in late 2005 of Afghanistan's democrati-

cally elected parliament, the first representative government in many, many decades, was immensely satisfying, especially to those who had any role in driving out the Soviets in the 1980s and ousting the Taliban in 2001 and 2002. The trouble is, of course, that although the politics have changed from totalitarian to democratic, the security situation remains challenging. Based in areas of Pakistan that even the redoubtable Pakistani army does not often venture, the Taliban—or more properly, its remnants—is apparently intent on reestablishing a presence inside Afghanistan and eventually retaking the country. It has even adopted the repellent tactic of suicide bombing to achieve its ends.

Afghanistan's drug trade, centered on the production of opium, is resurgent, thanks in part to the protection afforded by some warlords. As with any lucrative drug trade, the traffic in Afghanistan threatens the country's stability because the money it generates could corrupt government officials and the rule of law. Popular confidence in Afghanistan's budding democratic government could thus be undermined.

Another problem confronting the new Afghan government is the continuing power of the country's warlords. Many of these men, some of whom who have tried to remake themselves as more conventional politicians, are intent on building their political power through participation in the Afghan parliament while legitimizing their feudal positions in the Afghan countryside. Many of these warlords, however, have played an important role in the post-Taliban era. In 2001 and 2002, their forces were instrumental in driving out the Taliban and al-Qaeda; afterward, because there was no national army or police to speak of, they helped to stabilize the country and to prevent the survivors of Taliban and al-Qaeda from reestablishing themselves in southern and eastern Afghanistan. The challenge will be to persuade these warlords that the growing Afghan national army, numbering roughly 30,000 trained soldiers in early 2006, can and should assume a greater responsibility for the defense of the country while ensuring that the warlords' resources of men and weapons are at the disposal of the government in times of emergency.

Pakistan must be urged to act—assisted by Afghan and NATO forces within Afghanistan—to eliminate the al-Qaeda and Taliban presence from the "tribal" territories of Pakistan, the areas along the border. Destroying the Taliban and al-Qaeda would remove the greatest threat not only to Afghanistan but to the Pakistani government as well. Pakistan's intelligence service helped create the Taliban and see it into power. Now the Taliban is a threat to Pakistani political stability and progress.

Although the American military presence in Afghanistan is being reduced, our NATO allies, including Canada and the United Kingdom, are deploying more troops to Afghanistan and sending them to the areas where the Taliban is attempting to make a comeback. Just as encouraging is the continuing commitment of our allies to a necessary program of domestic improvements throughout the country. Currently, Provincial Reconstruction Teams (PRTs) are developing the areas outside of Kabul. Led by Americans, Germans, and workers from other NATO countries, the PRTs are proving to be very effective at planning, developing, and executing the reconstruction projects aimed at improving infrastructure, establishing schools, and restoring legitimate agriculture to attract some farmers away from growing opium poppies. Their operations as well as those of various aid agencies must be expanded—and protected— throughout the country. The Afghans must come to believe that the government in Kabul and its international allies are offering Afghanistan a better future. The key to ensuring a stable, peaceful Afghanistan is to stay the course. Allowing Afghanistan's economic and political development to languish and its security system to deteriorate would be to recreate the conditions that led to the establishment of the Taliban regime. We will likely be in Afghanistan, assisting in its development, for another ten to twenty years. But to defeat terrorism, we have no choice.

The force level that NATO needs to maintain in Afghanistan is relatively small, the duties in the long term, relatively easy. The fact that we will be keeping troops in Afghanistan (and other countries) for decades is not to say that the Web of Terror can't be defeated quickly. We defeated the Axis powers within four years of our entry into World War II—and yet we still have troops in German and Japan, sixty years later. So too in the war against terror we must act with a swift sword, as we did in Afghanistan, while recognizing that a longer-term military presence in the country is a necessary burden, and not an intolerable one.

Iraq

We were not at all surprised—and, in fact, predicted—that the Iraqi military would collapse rapidly in the face of the American-led coalition. We also are not entirely surprised at the failure of inspectors to find the weapons of mass destruction that every intelligence agency in the world believed that Saddam Hussein had. In the war against Islamist terror, we must act with a swift sword, as we did in Afghanistan, while recognizing that long-term military presences are necessary burdens and, if our allies can be convinced to take up some of the work at hand, hardly intolerable.

What already has been found in Iraq is an astonishing amount of conventional weapons in stockpiles throughout the country. In one unit's area of operations in Iraq, there were sixty-two ammunition supply points, one of which had more than 4,000 rocket-propelled grenades, along with other weapons and ammunition, in its inventory. One Army explosive ordnance disposal expert predicted that, using normal procedures, it would take *seventeen years* to get rid of the conventional weapons amassed by Saddam Hussein.

Another big surprise in Iraq is how "rotten" Iraq was by the spring of 2003. We knew that Saddam Hussein's military had been downgraded by years of sanctions; that is why we were confident the bulk of the Iraqi army would not put up much of a fight. What was a surprise was how thoroughly those decades of corruption and ineptitude on the part of Saddam Hussein and his cronies, and the years of economic sanctions against Iraq had hollowed out the country's infrastructure. Although Iraq's public infrastructure was not a target for coalition air-power, when coalition forces liberated Iraq, they found that the country's public utilities essentially were lashed together by baling wire and chewing gum.

And of course, the economy of Iraq was a mess. It was dilapidated to begin with. But the disruption of war and the disbanding of the Iraqi army brought the combined rate of underemployment and unemployment, according to one intelligence officer, to at least 60 percent and perhaps as high as 80 percent.

Although much more work remains before the Iraqi economy reaches its full potential, as with Afghanistan, the most pressing concern in Iraq will be security. Iraq has become the front line for the jihadists in their war against the West and moderate Islam. And it will remain a combat zone until the jihadists find their situation untenable. Part of that battle will be fought by us, part by the de-Ba'athified Iraqi police and army, and part by our reconstruction efforts that need to have as their objective providing full employment for the Iraqi people.

While we expect American forces to be deployed in Iraq for the next two decades, it will be an ever-shrinking number of troops. Indeed, we expect that in the end the U.S. presence will be directed at deterring Iranian and Syrian designs on Iraq as well as training Iraq's military, security, and police forces. We expect that as few as three or four Army and/or Marine brigades, together with a strong contingent of the U.S. Air Force, will be based in Iraq.

As of February 2004, there were up to 200,000 trained Iraqi security forces with a target number of 300,000, and probably more dependent upon the jihadist insurgency, by the end of 2004. These security forces are composed of the Army, Border Patrol, Police, Facility Protections Services, and Civil Defense forces. We agree that these numbers should be increased as scheduled to 300,000. This is a challenge, because many of these units will receive their final training "on the job," and because special care must be taken to ensure that Ba'athist diehards and radical Islamists do not infiltrate their ranks. Aggressive tactics—hunting down diehard antigovernment fighters, uncovering their caches of money and weapons, and denying them other sources of support—are what will keep the Ba'athists and jihadists off-balance. Our own troops can be more aggressive militarily if Iraqi forces are doing the internal security and police work as well as developing intelligence sources—tasks for which the Iraqis are better suited than are we, knowing as they do the people and the culture in ways that we can never hope to rival.

The Iraqi army and newly formed Iraqi border police need to be large enough to shut down Iraq's borders to the Ba'athists, the jihadists, and those who supply them with manpower and money. On some of Iraq's borders, the number of jihadists slipping across is relatively small. Our sources tell us that along Iraq's long border with Saudi Arabia perhaps only two or three a night, sometimes as many as five, come across (although in one incident, seventy-five jihadists were intercepted and killed). Once across, however, they can be hard to trace, because their contacts provide them with forged Iraqi identity papers. Iraqi soldiers and police officers could identify them as foreigners by their accents and methods of speech, but coalition troops are unlikely to note the differences. Even if the number of incoming jihadists is only a trickle, it still amounts to 60 to 150 fighters a month coming in from across the Saudi border alone, and adding a hundred terrorists a month to the already volatile situation in Iraq can mean a lot of trouble. But it shouldn't—because we have the technology to track down those trying to get into Iraq. We could significantly improve the surveillance of the border areas with high-technology observation equipment. Deploying such technology as the Global Hawk, the latest word in long-endurance, high-flying unmanned aerial vehicles (UAVs), can help prevent troublemakers from Iran, Syria, and Saudi Arabia from getting into Iraq.

We must also make the most of our efforts to restore "normal life" in Iraq, creating the conditions in which children can walk safely to school, electricity is reliable, and fresh, drinkable water comes out of every opened tap. Although we are making unheralded strides and achieving everyday victories in the restoration of public education and public services, that is only part of the job. The physical infrastructure of Iraq must be restored so that commerce can thrive. The big victory, however, will come when a democratic civil life—what Americans would consider "normal"—takes root and blooms in Iraq. When the Iraqis gain a stake in their own government through an electoral process that is stable and repeatable (they must avoid the "One Man–One Vote–One Time" trap), and when responsibility for public services, such as water and schools, lies with local authorities, our job in the country will be done. Iraq then will be ready to care for itself.

We are confident that the Iraqi people are up to the task, based on how enthusiastically they have embraced the opportunities to vote in meaningful elections. However, we do not underestimate the difficulties of building a lasting democracy and durable economy in Iraq. Iraq needs our support to guarantee the three S's: security, services, and salaries. As you might expect, these are interrelated tasks. Our military forces—with their presence, firepower, operations, and, most especially, training of Iraqi forces—can buttress the Iraqis' efforts to secure their country's infrastructure against acts of sabotage and other disruptions. As soon as the efficient delivery services—water, electricity, transportation, broadcasting—become commonplace through the work of the foreign corporations that are rebuilding and improving Iraq's infrastructure with job creation, there will be fewer grounds for political disaffection and greater cause for economic confidence. Given the county's large oil deposits, as soon as the oil production system has been restored and can be protected against sabotage, wealth will flow into the government's coffers that can be used to make even more improvements in Iraq's public services, which in turn will spur even more economic activity, especially by the Iraqi businesses, large and small, that are springing up all over that country. In short, a sound

Iraqi economy and thus a stable Iraqi social and civic life are very achievable goals.

There is a lot the United States and other nations can do to deliver jobs, an infrastructure that works, and public safety, and so strengthen the prospects for the rise of a stable, democratic Iraq. Just as important, however, there is one thing we *cannot* do: withdraw precipitately from Iraq. Having been on the scene, we know what it will take—and we know how much our work is valued. In September 2003, we traveled to the Persian Gulf for a weeklong Defense Department–sponsored trip. We spent much of the time in Iraq. Everywhere—*everywhere*—we went we encountered Iraqis who told us quite plainly how appreciative they were that the United States and its allies had overthrown Saddam Hussein and had given them the opportunity to develop a civil, democratic society. Yes, they were not happy about the lack of public services and the dearth of jobs, but they welcomed the opportunity to develop a democratic civil society. Repeatedly, the conversations would end with the Iraqi to whom we were speaking saying, "Thank you, America, for liberating us." We know from polls and press reports, our discussions with journalists (including our colleagues at FOX News Channel), diplomats, intelligence officers, and the men and women of our military that the Iraqi people want the coalition to stay.

On a broader strategic scale, a rapid withdrawal of American forces before Iraq is secure and stable would only underline our enemies' canard that the United States does not have the stomach for anything resembling a protracted struggle and undermine our credibility as an ally to those regimes in the region and around the world that might seek our assistance to repel radical Islamists' attempts to overthrown them.

Iran

In many aspects, Iran is a more formidable enemy than Iraq. It has a larger population, a more challenging terrain, and a military not degraded by years of sanctions. That said, Iran is very likely to fall more easily than Iraq did, because Iran's domestic opposition is developing into a serious threat to the regime.

Iran reminds us of the Soviet Union circa 1989. It is a large country with a huge population (more than sixty-eight million), and it should be a rich country, sitting as it does on huge reserves of oil. The country's wealth, however, does not make it down to the majority of Iranians. Instead, approximately 40 percent of Iranians live in poverty, because the clerics who control Iranian political and economic life siphon off much of the national income for their own uses.

The Constitution of the Soviet Union promised numerous rights to its citizens. Likewise, the Iranian constitution presents a façade of political freedom. It has an elected parliament and a democratically elected president. The catch, however, is that the constitution also vests all ultimate power in an nonelected body of six clerics and six religious lawyers, the Guardian Council, and the post of Supreme Ruler, a cleric chosen by another nonelected body, the House of Experts.

For many years, the Islamic Republic apparently was popular within Iran. However, over time, many Iranians have come to oppose the theocratic nature of the Iranian state and resent the concentration of political and economic power in the hands of the mullahs, their families, and their cronies. Among the youth of Iran there are many who find Western political forms and even elements of Western culture more attractive than the political and cultural construct offered by the mullahs. In fact, judging from recent political developments in Iran, it appears that the rule of the mullahs survives only because they manipulate Iran's political process. Democratic reform won't happen easily in Iran—because the mullahs and their allies are intent on keeping their positions of power by whatever means necessary, from manipulating the law to snuffing out political opposition, the quasi-official paramilitary forces at their command, their own versions of the militias and "fedayeen" of Ba'athist Iraq. It cannot be denied, however, that the people of Iran are ready and eager for it. The broadly popular Iranian movement in favor of democracy deserves our support for three simple reasons: the Iranian people want to be free, they deserve to be free, and the Web of Terror will greatly diminish when they are free.

For these reasons, the United States and other free nations should offer the democratic opposition everything we can to help them spread their message: satellite phones, computers, fax machines, even satellite radio and television stations, Voice of America broadcasts, and so on. Our goal should be to help the democratic opposition achieve the same impact on Iran that Solidarity had in Communist Poland. Our president should make it clear that our country stands behind the ambitions of the Iranian people for freedom. And if we succeed in creating a stable, democratic Iraq, the president's words will have a very tangible meaning for the people in Iran.

As encouraging as the growing strength of the pro-democracy movement in Iran is, we cannot wait for moral suasion and quiet diplomacy to have some effect on the mullahs. They are a key strand in the Web of Terror, and their nuclear ambitions are dangerously close to fulfillment.

The Iranians insist that their nuclear program is devoted to civilian purposes, to provide electricity. In September 2003, however, inspectors of the UN's International Atomic Energy Agency reported that they had discovered highly enriched (weapons-grade) uranium on equipment at an Iranian nuclear site. This discovery—and other reports concerning the Iranian nuclear program, including some that we heard directly from Israeli and Indian diplomats—brings into question the CIA's oft-cited analysis that Iran would have nuclear weapons in two to three *years*. We remember all too well the shock that occurred when, after the 1991 Persian Gulf War, international inspectors discovered that Saddam Hussein's nuclear program was much farther along than prewar intelligence estimates had claimed. We also now know—thanks to Libya's about-face on its WMD programs—that

Libya was much farther along in developing nuclear weapons than anyone imagined. There is no reason to be sanguine and there is every reason to be worried about how far Iran has gone and is going in its nuclear program.

If Iran develops nuclear weapons, so might other countries in the region. Saudi Arabia, for instance, already has as many as fifty Chinese-made intermediate-range ballistic missiles. Saudi Arabian officials have met with Pakistan's President Musharraf, and Pakistan has a history of selling nuclear technology and nuclear know-how, including apparently to Iran, North Korea, and Libya. We have no way of knowing what the Pakistani nuclear establishment might have sold to Riyadh in the way of equipment, advice, and documents related to nuclear weapons or the Pakistani army might have exchanged as a quid pro quo for Saudi financial support of the Taliban and Pakistan-sponsored Islamist rebels in Kashmir. It is imperative that Pakistan disclose all of its nuclear proliferation dealings with other countries.

More important is the question of Israel's reaction to Iran's nuclear weapons program. On January 4, 2004, the Israeli Defense Minister, Shaul Mofaz, an Iranian-born Israeli, spoke to the Iranian people via a radio broadcast. Speaking in his native Farsi, General Mofaz bluntly told his listeners that Israel would not accept an Iranian nuclear bomb. Only a couple of weeks later, we met with Israeli diplomats who underlined Mofaz's comments. In late 2005, Israel made clear that its defense staffs were drawing up a number of plans to strike Iran's nuclear facilities. There is precedent for such a strike. In 1981, in a brilliantly planned and executed attack, the Israeli Air Force destroyed Iraq's French-built Osirak nuclear reactor, an act that was publicly condemned and privately welcomed in the region and around the world.

Moreover, Iran continues to be a major state sponsor of terrorism with such clients as Hezbollah, Palestinian Islamic Jihad, and Yasser Arafat's Palestinian Authority. Iranian support of these groups is coordinated by agents of Iran's Ministry of Intelligence and Security

(MOIS) and the Iranian Revolutionary Guard Corps (also known as the Pasdaran), organizations that have been used by the mullahs to export Iranian-style Islamic revolution throughout the region for decades. In early January 2004, an American intelligence officer confirmed to us that there are also al-Qaeda operatives in Iran—and Iran has refused to turn over these terrorists to the United States.

A pro-Western, democratic regime in Iraq is, obviously, a threat to the Iranian mullahs' legitimacy because it would provide a rallying point for Iranian exiles and would-be democratic reformers. If the mullahs continue to run Iran, they will try to destroy a democratic Iraq. It was not a surprise, therefore, when we learned from a CIA officer that the MOIS already is active in the Shi'ite areas of Iraq, often in support of extremist Shi'ite clerics. We cannot tolerate Iranian support for terrorism, including attempts to subvert Iraq. But most of all, we cannot tolerate Iran's development of nuclear weapons.

The president must first inform Iran in the bluntest language possible that developing nuclear weapons is a red line it cannot cross. The president should not only immediately invoke his statutory authority to impose sanctions against corporations that do business with Iran's oil industry, but also encourage foreign governments to do the same. Japan needs to be encouraged to crack down on its corporations by a direct appeal to its self-interest: Every Japanese corporation that invests in Iran's oil industry is making a de facto investment in Iran's nuclear weapons cooperation with North Korea—and North Korea has Japan as a target. Likewise, the United States must urge Russia and Germany to pull their support from Iran's civilian nuclear program; the technology and know-how is too easily transferred to weapons programs. It might be worth approaching France with a request to restrict its support of Iran's nuclear program if only to give the world another example of the French government's boundless venality.

The United States must prepare to approach the UN Security Council with a draft resolution for a total economic embargo on Iran, the seizing of Iranian assets (to be held in trust for future Iranian government), and a strict naval quarantine in the Persian Gulf and the Strait of Hormuz. The United Nations would lift the embargo only when the Iran government dismantles its nuclear weapons program under the supervision of international inspections. Libya (and before Libya, South Africa) has given Iran an example to follow on how to dismantle a nuclear weapons program in a way that meets international standards of verification. Iran would be required to surrender or destroy all equipment needed to produce fissionable materials (highly enriched uranium and plutonium), all long-range ballistic missiles, and all cruise missiles; release all documents related to its nuclear weapons program; and expel all foreign scientists, technicians, and engineers involved in nuclear weapons design, development, and production. Because the French or Russians are likely to veto—or, at least, threaten to veto—such a Security Council resolution, the United States should be ready to impose these conditions on Iran with a coalition of our own. If that coalition is, in the end, composed solely of the United States, the Gulf States, Great Britain, Australia, Japan, and India, it would be enough.

A strict "no sanctuary" policy regarding terrorists is an essential part of the global strategy against terrorism. Therefore, the United States should be prepared to give Iran another dose of strong antiterror medicine by using airpower to strike terrorist sanctuaries within Iran. If Iran allows al-Qaeda or other jihadist groups to set up shop or take refuge within its borders, it must pay the price of being an accessory to and abettor of terrorism.

The Iranian mullahs' support for terrorism, their repression of their own people who so obviously yearn to be free, and their appalling human rights record are reasons enough to change the regime. Their ambitious nuclear weapons program makes regime change in Iran more than desirable; it makes it necessary—now. And to achieve that, we should deploy every lever we have—diplomatic, economic, and even military—until we get the necessary result.

North Korea

North Korea created its nuclear weapons program for money, which means, *for export.* North Korean scientists, engineers, and technicians are in Tehran and other cities in Iran, working for Iran's nuclear weapons program. North Korea is developing and selling ballistic missiles to Iran, Syria, and Yemen (and probably to other customers that we might not know about now). Pakistan has admitted that it traded its expertise related to nuclear weapons to North Korea for North Korea's expertise in ballistic missile technology.

In an August 5, 2003, op-ed in the *Wall Street Journal,* Jim Woolsey, former director of the CIA, and Tom wrote a lengthy article on resolving the problems with North Korea. In it they describe how the North Koreans use their nuclear weapons program *for extortion.* Not only has North Korea violated agreements not to pursue nuclear weapons and withdrawn from the Nuclear Non-Proliferation Treaty, it has demanded what is essentially a bribe to turn the program off again. North Korea expects that if it rattles its nuclear weapons and ballistic missiles enough, it will succeed, as it has in the past, in shaking money and material aid from the United States and Japan. Its transparently mercenary motives, however, shouldn't disguise the fact that the North Korean nuclear threat is very real.

In early July 2003, krypton 85—a gas produced when spent nuclear fuel is reprocessed into plutonium for nuclear weapons—was detected in an area removed from North Korea's only known reprocessing facility at Yongbyon. In January 2004, North Korea showed an unofficial delegation of American nuclear experts who were touring its nuclear facilities that it removed spent fuel rods from the holding ponds where earlier nuclear inspectors had put them and sent them away for "reprocessing." When North Korea ousted international inspectors and left the Nuclear Non-Proliferation Treaty in January 2002, it had 8,000 spent fuel rods at the Yongbyon facility. If they indeed have been reprocessed, North Korea's dictator Kim Jong Il might have material for several nuclear weapons (he is already suspected of having one or two).

The news gets worse. In the fall of 2003, the CIA declared that North Korea's nuclear weapons program is sufficiently sophisticated that it will not have to explode a nuclear bomb in order to determine if its weapons will work. That means that the world might not know North Korea has operational weapons until it actually uses one, or another rogue state or a terrorist group detonates one of the weapons North Korea has sold it in Los Angeles, Tel Aviv, New Delhi, or London. Given North Korea's boast in April 2003 that it would sell weapons-grade plutonium to whomever it pleased, there is no gainsaying the fact that the North Korean nuclear threat is enormous and pressing.

There is no realistic way to stop North Korea from exporting plutonium—and even manufactured weapons—to potential customers, which would include rogue states and terrorist organizations. North Korea already clandestinely ships ballistic missiles to customers all over the world. Former Secretary of Defense William Perry observed that the amount of plutonium needed for a bomb is about the size of a soccer ball. It would be easy for the North Koreans to use air shipments, including those protected by diplomatic immunity, to smuggle nuclear materials and/or bomb components to their customers.

So how do we stop North Korea? There are two options. First, North Korea is dependent on China for food, fuel, and financial support. China needs to understand that if North Korea goes ahead with its nuclear weapons program, then Japan, Taiwan, and even South Korea could follow—and Northeast Asia would be "nuclearized." The president of the United States should remind the Chinese that this scenario is not in their interest, and remind them too that he and South Korea's president, Roh Moo-hyun, signed a joint declaration in May 2003 that they will "not tolerate nuclear weapons in North Korea."

The Chinese might eschew such a forceful course of action—as they have in the past. North Korea is their ally after all. Or China might demand concessions related to Taiwan that the United States would find intolerable. That means the United States needs to develop other options. Many U.S. policymakers reflexively reject the use of force against North Korea, casting any conflict on the Korean peninsula in nightmarish terms. The Chinese and North Koreans know this, and take advantage of it. To put it bluntly, they do not expect American action. To restore our diplomatic credibility and to have an effective response if war becomes unavoidable, however, the United States and South Korea must come together—initially in secret, if necessary— and begin to assess realistically what it would take to change the North Korean regime by military means.

A surgical strike against the nuclear site at Yongbyon would be insufficient, not only because there might be other nuclear sites, but because we must protect South Korea from attack, particularly from the masses of North Korean artillery just north of the Demilitarized Zone. We must prepare to win a war, not merely execute a strike.

To our advantage, the U.S. and South Korean militaries have spent more than fifty years preparing to fight and win a war against North Korea. Massive airpower is the key to being able both to destroy Yongbyon and to protect South Korea from attack by missiles or artillery. There are many hardened air bases available in South Korea, and the South Koreans have an excellent air force of approximately 550 modern tactical aircraft.

The United States should begin planning to deploy the Patriot tactical ballistic missile defense system in South Korea. We should also deploy U.S. Navy warships equipped with the Aegis system to shoot down ballistic missiles fired at South Korea and Japan. The United States also should reinforce its tactical air forces in the area, moving several air wings to Japan and South Korea, putting aircraft carrier battle groups in the Western Pacific, and deploying surveillance aircraft and drones.

All these elements must be movable on short notice in order that, once "the balloon goes up" in Korea, that U.S. and South Korean air forces can launch well over 4,000 sorties a day (compared with 800 in Iraq). Considering that the vast majority of these sorties would use precision munitions, and that surveillance aircraft would permit immediate targeting of artillery pieces and ballistic missile launch sites, the use of air power in such a war would be swifter and more devastating than it was in Iraq.

North Korea's obsolescent air defenses—both fighter aircraft and ground-based missiles—would not last long. Most of North Korea's armed forces are along the DMZ. Smash them in a ferocious air campaign and the rest of the country is open to ground operations by U.S. and South Korean forces. Marine forces deployed off both coasts of North Korea could put both Pyongyang and Wonsan at risk of rapid seizure, particularly given the fact that most of North Korea's armed forces are situated along the DMZ.

In addition, the South Korean army is well equipped and well trained. With help from perhaps two additional U.S. Army divisions, it could drive quickly and deeply into North Korea. In fact, our combined forces could defeat North Korea decisively in thirty to sixty days. There is no doubt on the outcome. If North Korea refuses to end its nuclear program—and if China refuses to force North Korea to end it—we need to make it clear that we will act decisively to take out North Korea's weapons and its noxious regime. We can and we must.

Syria

Syria is a domino waiting to fall. It is an enormous supporter of terrorism—but it lacks the oil wealth of Iran, Saudi Arabia, Libya, and Iraq. It is a ruthless police state—but its base of support is Alawite Muslims, who make up about 11 percent of the population. It is the last Ba'ath Party–controlled state; its deep-pocketed Ba'athist neighbor, Saddam Hussein, is gone.

And most important for us are reports that Saddam Hussein sent chemical, biological, and other weapons or weapons components to three locations in Syria. The first is in northern Syria in a tunnel complex used by the Syrians for their own WMD called al Baida. The second location is a Syrian Air Force Camp near Tai Snan. The third location is in southern Syria, near the Lebanese border, in a city called Sjinsjam, itself close to the city of Homs. Weapons also could be hidden in sites in the Bekaa Valley. Saddam Hussein and his henchmen sent these weapons as well as hundreds of millions of dollars in cash to Syria for "safekeeping." With Saddam Hussein's regime gone, cash-strapped Syria undoubtedly kept the cash and weapons. It can use the money to prop up the regime and will use the weapons to support its new sponsor, Iran. The success of Hamas in the 2006 Palestinian elections makes this even more likely. Israel would be the target. Israel knows the weapons are present in Syria, and, therefore, we would not be surprised to see preemptive Israeli strikes against Syria to prevent these weapons from being transferred to these terrorist groups.

Immediately after Operation Iraqi Freedom, Syria made diplomatic overtures to the West. Then, it seemed to us, the Syrian regime was making a sound decision. Its geostrategic, economic, and diplomatic positions were weak and the regime knew that it had little popular support. While impressive to some on paper, Syria's military is unimpressive in reality.

Syria, however, soon tired of its double game—and emboldened by tacit and tangible support from Iran—returned to its usual intransigence. Terror groups, such as Hamas, still are allowed to maintain a presence there. Although popular outrage at Syria's involvement in the assassination of former Lebanese prime minister Rafik Hariri eventually led to a withdrawal of the Syrian army and intelligence services from Lebanon, Syria seems intent on maintaining as much influence as possible over the country. It is not at all squeamish about using extreme means to do so. Assassinations—all bearing the mark of Syria—have killed a number of prominent Lebanese politicians and journalists and caused a number of high-profile Lebanese political leaders to seek refuge outside the country.

Gone, too, is all talk of accommodation with the West and Israel. Syrian leaders have conducted open and well-publicized meetings with Iranian leaders, openly supported jihadists going into Iraq, and mounted a robust public relations effort aimed at buttressing popular support for the regime. To us, all of this communicates a message of pure defiance from President Bashar Assad and his cronies, an indication that they are confident that they have weathered the worst, that the United States and its allies are concentrated on Iraq, and that they can conduct business as usual without fear of confrontation.

The havoc in the region caused by Syria as well as the knowledge that its discomfiture will be felt by its patron, Iran, are reasons enough for the United States to end Syria's double game immediately by issuing an ultimatum to Syria's president, Bashar Assad: expel all terror groups from Syrian soil and Syrian-controlled Lebanon, give up all Iraqi weapons of mass destruction, and stop letting Iranian cadres, weapons, and money pass through your country to Palestinian terror groups—or the United States and a coalition of the willing will topple your regime.

Facing the Mediterranean Sea, Syria is an ideal place to use America's dominant sea and air power. Coalition forces would move quickly into Syria and the Bekaa Valley, guiding precision air strikes on terrorist training camps, harassing any terrorists who flee U.S. air assaults, and seeking storage sites for weapons of mass destruction. Delivering reinforcements quickly at key points would be a relatively simple affair.

Bashar Assad should be made to realize that he has two options: cooperate with the civilized world against terror, as Colonel Gaddafi is apparently doing, or be toppled like Saddam Hussein.

Saudi Arabia

The House of Saud remains locked in a battle against Islamist terror.

Since May 2003, al-Qaeda has fought against the Saudi regime, attacking compounds that housed foreign workers essential to the Saudi economy.

To their credit, the Saudi security forces have pursued the terrorists relentlessly, killing many in ferocious gun battles, and arrested hundreds of suspected al-Qaeda operatives and their supporters. The Saudi authorities also have uncovered large caches of arms as well as bundles of documents related to al-Qaeda's financial records.

Al-Qaeda has many fighters and supporters within Saudi Arabia. As one analyst told us, only about 25 percent of the Saudi population wholeheartedly supports the royal family. Ironically, the inflexible Wahhabi Islam preached by Saudi-funded clerics in mosques, taught in Saudi-funded schools, and put into action by Saudi-supported Islamist groups around the world is what inspires the anti-monarchist forces. The chickens have come home to roost for the House of Saud. It now is fighting the very terrorism that it helped create.

That might seem poetic justice to some, but the United States has an interest in Saudi reform rather than revolution. In the late 1970s, the United States stood by while the Shah of Iran fell and an Islamic republic took his place. That foreign policy mistake gave rise to the mullahs and eventually the Web of Terror that constitutes the greatest post-Communist threat to the Western world. The United States, therefore, cannot make the same mistake in Saudi Arabia that it did in Iran. We cannot let anti-American mullahs replace another monarchy in the Persian Gulf region.

The House of Saud is a seething mess of competing factions—and, therefore, the Kingdom's government often seems to be of two minds (at least), with some of its members assuring the West that it stands with it against terrorism as others pursue those policies that help spread the stern Wahhabi Islam that often drives Islamist terror. The infuriating fact remains, however, that, in the short term at least, the United States must support the House of Saud. We must continue to provide material assistance and training to the Saudi military and the kingdom's security forces in their now almost daily battles with Islamist terrorists.

That said, it is time for the United States to put the House of Saud on notice. Business as usual isn't good enough. The Kingdom's recent tough response to domestic terrorism—striking with "an iron fist," as the Crown Prince colorfully puts it—is an admirable one; as the Shah discovered in 1979, however, that can only go so far in preserving a dynasty. The Kingdom needs to reform its economy, domestic politics, and foreign policy immediately.

The president should be clear: Saudi Arabia must close "the Islamic interests" section in every Saudi Arabian embassy and stop its support and promotion of Islamic schools and mosques that promote Wahhabi Islam, Islamic "charities," and other incubators of terror. For too long, the House of Saud has assumed that by funding radical Islam it could tame and divert it. In fact, the Saudis have a created a monster that threatens the Islamic world and the West and now the monarchy itself. The Kingdom of Saudi Arabia spends hundreds of millions of dollars a year supporting radical Wahhabi Islam around the world, funding terrorist groups like Palestinian Islamic Jihad and Hamas, and making payments to the families of Palestinian suicide bombers. This money should be better spent reforming the Saudi education system so that it teaches job skills, not hatred of "infidels." Saudi Arabia's neighbor, Qatar, provides a perfect model for reform of the Saudi education system. In 2003, under the sponsorship of the Emir of Qatar and his wife, Qatar established "Education City," a 2,400-acre facility in cooperation with such institutions as Texas A&M, Cornell University Medical School, and the Rand Corporation. Not only do the institutions of "Education City" offer schooling, they spur research and development that can improve the quality of life for the people. Soon, the Qatar government will begin a reform of its elementary and secondary education system. One of its specific goals is to develop an appreciation of other cultures and religions, to foster tolerance and understanding, rather than hatred and terrorism. If Saudi Arabia—with its much greater wealth—followed Qatar's lead, it could become *the* major center of learning *in all disciplines* (not just in Wahhabi theology), in the Arab world, indeed in the Islamic world.

As the Shah of Iran discovered in the late 1970s, however, establishing a quality education system is not enough. There must be jobs for the well-educated graduates. And that means reforming Saudi Arabia's economy so that it is no longer almost solely dependent on the extraction of mineral wealth, but is a diversified market economy from which Saudi Arabia can derive widespread economic prosperity as other Gulf States—like Qatar, Bahrain, Dubai, and Abu Dhabi—have done. Taking a cue from other Muslim monarchies, such as Morocco, Qatar, and Bahrain, the leadership of Saudi Arabia should begin the process of transforming the kingdom's political system from a family business into a constitutional monarchy, complete with a written constitution and a sound and open legal system in which any citizen can expect justice. If the House of Saud persists in treating Saudi Arabia as a family possession run solely for the family's benefit, the dynasty's future will be imperiled, no matter how successful its current crackdown against internal terrorism.

If the House of Saud does not follow an American diplomatic lead to reform along the lines we've sketched, it could easily fall to an Islamist revolution. So the United States must dust off the contingency plans to meet that threat, which would mean invading Saudi Arabia, seizing its oil fields, production facilities, and tanker terminals, securing and isolating them from the Islamists—and defeating them with the assistance of the more Western-oriented princes, who need to be identified now, who can lead a counterrevolutionary opposition. Other Gulf States, like Qatar and Kuwait, would certainly come to our aid.

On the subject of Saudi Arabia, two words are enough to prevent some U.S. policymakers from acting aggressively to save the regime: *Mecca* and *Medina*, the two holiest cities in Islam. The presence of American forces in Saudi Arabia inflamed Osama bin Laden and prompted the Khobar Towers bombing. But a radical Islamic takeover would be worse than any reaction to American troops in Saudi Arabia.

With the help of the other Gulf States and with reformist pro-Western Saudi princes, we can turn back that terrorist threat.

Pakistan

Although President Pervez Musharraf has survived at least two assassination attempts, Pakistan still balances on a razor's edge. Like Saudi Arabia, Pakistan is divided between a pro-Western faction and a large and powerful Islamist faction. Pakistan considers itself a leading Islamic country. Its constitution enshrines sharia law. It has the only Islamic nuclear weapon—so far. And, unfortunately, many within Pakistan, including some in its army and military intelligence service, supported the Taliban, which is now regrouping in the tribal areas of Pakistan along the Afghan border. Despite the declarations of President Musharraf after the London 2005 terrorist attacks, some of which had been carried out by young Britons who had spent time in Pakistani madrassas, the country's religious schools continue to indoctrinate masses of students in the doctrines of radical Islam. And Pakistani nuclear scientists have made the rounds of rogue states, selling equipment and technical expertise to advance their nuclear weapons programs. Pakistan's future depends on its willingness to confront the Taliban, al-Qaeda, and other Islamist terrorist and terror-supporting groups within its own borders.

President Bush must press President Musharraf to continue investigating—and to halt—the "private" activities of Pakistani nuclear scientists, which it appears he has done with the admission of guilt by A.Q. Khan. Such activities have resulted in nuclear weapons knowledge going to Iran and North Korea. The United States needs to know the full extent and details of these breaches of security, so that we can have a better idea of how far developed are the nuclear weapons programs of these rogue states.

In the probable absence of an Indo-Pakistani nuclear disarmament treaty, the United States and the United Kingdom could offer Pakistan an agreement in which Pakistan would strictly and effectively prohibit its nuclear establishment from engaging in any activities that would advance nuclear proliferation and, in exchange, the United States and the United Kingdom would provide increased economic and military aid to Pakistan.

Another important step for President Musharraf while he retains the post of army chief of staff is to purge the army of any radical Islamist influences. The Pakistani army is the only national institution that has both the brains *and* the brawn to control Pakistan. Turkey's military is the guarantor of a secular, democratic Turkey. Musharraf needs to follow the Turkish model and make the Pakistani army a bulwark against the radical Islamists. Moreover, he needs to reorganize Pakistan's Inter-Service Intelligence (ISI), the military intelligence service that is best known for organizing, training, and arming the mujahideen in Afghanistan during the 1980s. Unfortunately, it also has been linked to terrorism in Indian-held Kashmir and is credited with being the organizing force behind the Taliban. The ISI has outlived its usefulness to Pakistan, and if allowed to exist in its present form, has the potential to destabilize Pakistan as well as other countries in South and Central Asia.

Related to reorganizing the ISI, Pakistan must eliminate the remnants of al-Qaeda and the Taliban from within its own borders. If President Musharraf asks for assistance in this effort, we must be willing to provide everything from intelligence to air strikes, from transportation to conventional ground forces. It is risky for Musharraf to act, but our diplomats need to point out that it is riskier for him not to act— and that we will support him. Finally, we have to think of how we would deal with the consequences of the unthinkable: the overthrow or assassination of President Musharraf and perhaps a consequent civil war with the ultimate prize being nuclear weapons, ballistic missiles, and the infrastructure to build more of them. America should work closely to safeguard Pakistan's nuclear arsenal and keep nuclear warheads from falling under control of rogue commanders or Islamic terrorists. We should be prepared to give them U.S. technology that will prevent Pakistan from launching its nuclear weapons by rogue elements.

Israel-Palestine

In the days preceding the Palestinian legislative elections in January 2006, the foreign policy establishment in the United States—the retired diplomats, the commentators, the academics, and the denizens of the think tanks—assured each other and the public that the elections could have only one outcome: a victory for Fatah, the political party founded by the archetypal terrorist leader of our age, Yasser Arafat.

As it turned out, the political wing of Hamas, the bloodthirsty, Iran-backed terrorist group that has committed numerous atrocities against Israel—including a large number of suicide bombings—routed Fatah at the polls, winning 74 of 132 seats in the Palestinian legislature. Afterward, the experts expressed astonishment at Hamas' victory, and the press echoed that astonishment.

To us, the success enjoyed by Hamas was no surprise, because we kept abreast of the situation in Israel through our friends and colleagues in Israel and at the FOX News Channel—people who do not let their daydreams cloud their analyses. From these sources, we knew that Fatah is essentially a criminal enterprise masking itself as a revolutionary nationalist and, when it suited it, Islamist movement (in the Cold War, such organizations described themselves as "national liberation movements"). Its leaders had their critics intimidated into silence or killed and helped themselves to billions of dollars that various governments—including the United States'—poured into its coffers. Taking their cue from their leaders, its lower-level operatives, especially those in armed units, shook down their neighbors and numerous government functionaries. (How much respect do you expect people to have for a government that can't stand up to its own gunmen?) All the while, the vast majority of the Palestinian people remained mired in poverty and misery, but expected to send sons

(and, recently, daughters) on suicide missions. It was a tottering criminal enterprise, hollowed out by corruption, incompetence, and internal rivalries.

Relative to Fatah and its representatives in the Palestinian Authority, Hamas is disciplined enough to focus its violent actions almost
exclusively against Israel (although it too intimidates and kills its
internal opponents), and is apparently interested enough in the wel-
fare of the Palestinian people to run various social services such as
schools, day care centers, and health clinics. In short, in the choice
between Fatah and Hamas, the Palestinians had a choice between corruption and virtue, chaos and discipline. Given those choices, it is
hardly surprising the majority chose Hamas.

Fatah also was the victim of its own propaganda success. For
decades, its media organs spewed vile and poisonous propaganda
against Israel and the West (especially the United States) meant to rad-
icalize an entire people, to ensure they would support and send their
children to participate in a sustained terror campaign against Israel. It
worked: surveys of Palestinians show that they are radicalized, that
they hate Israel and want to see it destroyed, that they despise the
United States. Why else would have thousands of Palestinians spon-
taneously celebrated the attacks of September 11?

Undoubtedly, Fatah is a terrorist organization. However, just as
Arafat would decry terrorist attacks in English in the morning and celebrate them in Arabic in the afternoon, after Arafat's death Fatah tried
to have it both ways. It posed as a legitimate national government to
much of the outside world—especially the Western nations and international organizations that bankrolled it—and as a revolutionary organization dedicated to Israel's destruction and the murder of Israelis to
its own people. Unfortunately, none of Fatah's new leadership had
anything approaching Arafat's status (which is just the way Arafat
wanted it) and without his credibility lacked the ability to pull off
this trick. The Palestinian people—steeped for years in strident anti-
Israel, pro-terrorist propaganda—had to choose between a party fully

committed to the "Death to Israel" propaganda line and a party that cynically tried to play both sides.

The same holds true on the issue of Islamism. Whenever Fatah flew the banner of Islamism, it always seemed to be a flag of convenience, something it hoisted to ensure that millions of dollars kept flowing in from Muslim countries. This was a crucial task after Fatah's former main sponsors, the Soviet Union and its satellites, changed their politics. Like Hezbollah in Lebanon, however, Hamas always has been committed to advancing radical Islamism (including forcing Palestinian Christians into second-class status). Is it any wonder that when choosing between two Islamist parties, the Palestinians chose the real one?

In February 2006, Hamas took control of the Palestinian Authority—and almost immediately announced that it would not waver from its commitment to the destruction of Israel and would not meet with Israeli officials. Many Western "experts," including many of those who confidently predicted a Fatah victory only a month before, began to expect that the demands of governing the Gaza Strip and other Palestinian areas (now collectively described by some wags as "Hamasistan") would "moderate" Hamas.

This thinking probably stems from the foreign policy establishment's article of faith that the settlement of the Israeli–Palestinian question is the key to peace throughout the Middle East. Give the Palestinians a homeland of their own and immediately peace will descend on the Middle East; radical Islam and terrorism will lose their appeal; and the lion will lie down with the lamb. All this is a dream—a self-defeating, nonsensical dream.

Unfortunately, this dream has immense power. It is the conventional wisdom—and provides a convenient excuse for inaction—in many capitals around the world. It is what may prompt many countries in the West to reject the U.S. call to cut off financial aid to Hamas and to urge Israel to give the Hamas-dominated Palestinian Authority a chance.

The Israelis already understand what the rest of the world needs to understand: that a negotiated settlement with Hamas is a pipe dream. In February 2006, Yuval Diskin, the head of Israel's internal security service, told the Knesset's foreign affairs and defense committee, "A Hamas state... will be a radical Sunni state that radical forces can reach from around the world.... A Hamas state like this, with terror and military capabilities, is a strategic threat to Israel." The Israelis also know that the terror campaign against them will not end if they cede all the land Israel won in the 1967 Six-Day War. A Palestinian state run by the likes of Hamas and closely allied with Syria and Iran will not be "a partner for peace," but an implacable enemy. Liberation will begin when the Palestinian terror complex is cut off from its outside support—Syria, Iran, and Saudi Arabia are the chief culprits— and the terrorists are then given a choice: total war, which they will lose, or real peace. Put another way, the current policy relies on an *inside out* solution; our solution is to approach the problem from the *outside in.* The dictatorships of Syria and Iran should be toppled and the Kingdom of Saudi Arabia should be reformed, as we've outlined.

The only way for a peaceful Palestinian state to emerge and for Israelis and Palestinians to live in a more hopeful future is to free the Palestinians from the totalitarians who rule them by the gun and the bomb and who have committed them to the genocidal goal of eliminating Israel and driving the Israelis into the sea. If the Palestinian people are ever to live in peace and in concord with their Israeli neighbors, if Palestinian children are ever to dream of becoming something else than a suicide bomber or a gunman, if Palestinian Christians are to sustain their faith and their presence in their homeland, then Palestinans need *liberation* from their terrorist masters. It is a gamble worth taking. Today, the Palestinians and the Israelis are living in intolerable conditions. The Palestinians are now governed by terrorists who are committed to Israel's destruction. The Israelis are forced to live lives in constant fear. To allow this situation to continue, to allow it to continue to serve as a rallying point for radical

Islamic terror, is tantamount to criminal neglect. The risk is worth the
likely gain.

THE GLOBAL WAR

We know the country-by-country strategy that we have outlined to
end the Web of Terror might sound daunting, but it can be done. And
it must be done. Al-Qaeda has a global presence. It is active in the
Middle East and North Africa. It is increasingly active in Central Asia
and Eastern Europe. It has cells in the West. It is active in Southeast
Asia, Indonesia, and the Philippines. And it is in East Africa. America is fighting al-Qaeda, globally, and we are winning. But victory
requires more than killing al-Qaeda's terrorists and freezing their
accounts.

When World War II began for the United States after Pearl Harbor,
our nation understood it had to defeat a great threat to world peace.
Today we face another such threat, after the Pearl Harbor of September 11, 2001. We will achieve victory again. With the tools our nation
has now, we can do it and, in relative terms, more easily than we did
almost sixty years ago. And the stakes are just as high.

We can act now and win, or we can wait and let the danger grow—
grow into the nightmare scenarios we sketched earlier. Any commander in chief who chooses the latter course has violated his obligation
to defend the people of the United States. President Clinton's refusal
to act in a decisive way against the murderous attacks by al-Qaeda
against Americans overseas emboldened the terrorist to launch the
September 11 attacks. No American president should make that mistake again. Declared enemies of the United States must be taken at
their word. If not cooperative and they remain defiant, our message
in response to them should be manifest: We will not tolerate your
support of terrorism, and your regime will be changed unless you
cooperate.

CHAPTER FOUR

INTO BATTLE: OPERATION ENDURING FREEDOM

I N LATE 2005, President Hamid Karzai of Afghanistan presided over the opening session of Afghanistan's new parliament. The Afghan constitution provided for a democratic republic centered on a two-house parliament, a supreme court system, and a directly elected presidency; guarantees basic political and civil rights; establishes that women are equal in the eyes of the law; and, in writing at least, squares this with the ideal of Afghanistan being an Islamic Republic with no laws being contrary to Islam.

It is still amazing to realize that in September 2001, Afghanistan was still controlled by the Taliban and was a base of several al-Qaeda operations, including the attacks on New York and Washington. Although there remains much work to secure Afghanistan against a resurgence of the Taliban, restore its economy, and rebuild its infrastructure, the outlook for Afghanistan is brighter than it has ever been in modern history. This was America's first victory against the Web of Terror. The speed with which the Bush administration organized and executed this counterstroke to the outrage of September 11 was remarkable. Also remarkable was that this was the first time the United States matched our enemies' militant rhetoric of a global jihad with an equally militant response.

For the terrorists associated with Osama bin Laden's terrorist conglomerate, Afghanistan was a secure base for rest and recuperation, training, recruitment, and money laundering. By September 2001, the al-Qaeda terrorists—Chechens, Arabs, Egyptians, and Pakistanis—were the Taliban's "palace guard." Their arrogant attitude and brutal behavior toward most Afghans made these "Arabs," as the Afghan people referred to them, widely loathed. The interdependence of the Taliban and al-Qaeda meant that the only way to rob al-Qaeda of its sanctuary in Afghanistan was to topple the regime that sheltered it.

Bringing down the Taliban was an obvious goal for other, broader reasons. It set out as a matter of U.S. policy the denial of sanctuaries to terrorists no matter where they were and no matter who gave them protection. Terrorists would know that whether they were in sight of the Hindu Kush or under the jungle canopy of the southern Philippines they would be pursued relentlessly and pitilessly. Governments that gave shelter to terrorists were put on notice: the United States would bring them down.

The first air attacks on the Taliban/al-Qaeda targets in Afghanistan were on October 7, 2001. American diplomats, intelligence personnel on the ground, and Bush administration leaders had paved the way by the diplomatic coup of securing flyover and basing rights in countries bordering Afghanistan—Uzbekistan, Tajikistan, and Pakistan—and receiving permission from many other countries (including the Persian Gulf states of Oman, Bahrain, and Kuwait) to place our forces on their soil. As is so often the case, the Kingdom of Saudi Arabia needed special handling. U.S. Central Command was keen to use the massive Prince Sultan Air Force Base, from which many strikes had flown against Iraq during the 1991 Gulf War. For reasons still unknown, the Saudis declined to allow aircraft to utilize Prince Sultan Air Force Base for strikes against the Taliban and al-Qaeda, but allowed its use as a command-and-control center. As to securing the bases in the Gulf, it was fortunate that Operation Southern Watch (patrolling the southern no-fly zone in Iraq) had been going on for a decade; it had given us invaluable experience in conducting sustained aerial operations at the end of a logistics line many thousands of miles long.

A diplomatic effort that we examined warily was the U.S. government's offer to the Taliban: surrender Osama bin Laden and we will let your regime stand. We were convinced that the Taliban needed to be dealt with, in any event, and we worried that Mullah Omar and others might stall for time while Osama bin Laden and his al-Qaeda command structure escaped. The Taliban, however, made the enormous miscalculation—as did much of world's media—that they could repel a U.S. assault. One media outlet that didn't make that mistake was FOX News Channel, where we were posted as military analysts.

We were grateful for NATO's declaration that the attack on a member country, the United States, demanded a military response. We were grateful that the Vatican lent its moral authority to Operation Enduring Freedom, by endorsing the right of self-defense as applied to the United States against al-Qaeda and the Taliban. We approved the sweeps that law enforcement and internal security organizations made in such countries as France, Germany, Spain, and Italy, actions often based on information provided by the United States.

There was another diplomatic effort, however, that we wish had happened, but didn't, which was for the president to seek a UN Security Council mandate to dismantle the entire Web of Terror. The administration quickly pieced together that the Web existed, that al-Qaeda was an isolated problem. President Bush made this official in his State of the Union speech in 2002 with his identification of the "Axis of Evil." But what would have been even more useful would have been a push in the UN Security Council for a declaration that all state sponsors of terror would be subjects of a possible UN-mandated military response in order to restore international security, law, and peace. There was a precedent for such a declaration, in part at least, with the UN-supported war against North Korean aggression, fifty years earlier. If the United States had pushed for such a resolution in late September 2001, it might very well have passed—as a symbol of moral support if nothing else—and such a resolution might have meant that

Saddam Hussein could have been removed as early as the fall of 2002, rather than well into April 2003 after fruitless diplomatic delays.

In our role as military analysts at FOX News Channel, we tried not only to provide strategic and tactical analysis, but to use our military experience to bust some of the myths that civilian reporters fell prey to. When reporters warned about the "harsh Afghan winter," we countered by saying that bad weather cuts both ways and that our forces had superior equipment for moving and fighting in cold weather. Some commentators warned that if we took action against the Taliban and al-Qaeda, thousands of nationalist Afghans would pick up their assault rifles and machine guns, flock to the Taliban's banner, and fight to repel the foreign invaders. We retorted that loyalties in Afghanistan often were more a matter of tribalism than nationalism and that the Taliban and al-Qaeda were widely hated. Many "experts" opined that Afghanistan was an unconquerable land defended by invincible fighters. In reply, we recalled that it had in fact been conquered by the British, the Russians (who withdrew in 1989 only when they decided it wasn't worth the cost), and indeed by the Taliban itself, which was an armed faction that had taken the country, albeit with support from Pakistan's Inter-Service Intelligence (ISI). The courage and fighting prowess of Afghan warriors, often referred to as the mujahideen, was legendary, but the Afghan fighting men were not indestructible—and more important, they were prone to switch sides if it seemed like a good thing to do.

We were not worried about the Taliban and al-Qaeda as a military force—what worried us was how our own generals might approach the task. During his tenure as chairman of the Joint Chiefs of Staff during the late 1980s and 1990s, Colin Powell had articulated "the Powell Doctrine," which had enormous, if unofficial, influence on American military thinking. A central tenet of that "doctrine" was that whenever and wherever the United States sent troops into battle, it had to deploy a numerically overwhelming force. Some compared the doctrine to using a jackhammer to open a walnut, but to others, the

Persian Gulf War of 1991 with its "100 Hour War" on the ground seemed to bear out Powell's vision.

In our experience, if an Army general (and not a few Marine generals) were asked what constitutes "overwhelming force," he would describe a heavy mechanized force—tanks, armored fighting vehicles, and self-propelled artillery. Moving U.S. Army divisions, even light ones, into a landlocked, mountainous country would be cutting out a massive piece of work for the Army and other services.

Initially, this massive force would have to move almost entirely by air. The power of Islamist political parties in Pakistan being what they were—and are—moving it across that country by land would have been asking the government of General Pervez Musharraf (still a largely unknown character) to take an enormous political risk. Considering that the Taliban and al-Qaeda were active in the provinces that bordered Afghanistan and had recruited young men to fight for them from the *madrassas* of those regions, any U.S. force moving through those provinces would have had enormous security problems and an unsecured supply line.

Moving heavy forces by air, however, is notoriously inefficient. The only transport aircraft capable of lifting the Army's 72-ton M-1 Abrams tank are the C-5A and C-17. Even if the way had been cleared to move the equipment sets of three divisions to Turkey by sea, before transporting them to the Incirlik air base in northern Turkey by land, and then moving them by air, deploying a force that large would have taken months. Equipment cannot just be dumped on the ground; it must be maintained, armed, and fueled, and that means maintenance facilities, fuel depots, and ammunition dumps must be established. Advanced communications networks and headquarters facilities are essential to wage modern warfare. Although there were some old Soviet bases in such places as Uzbekistan, the United States military would have had to establish modern facilities by building them from scratch. Even if the forces began arriving in late September 2001, there would be little chance for the force to begin operations before the spring of 2002.

In the time that the buildup was going on, the Taliban might have received more aid from Pakistan's ISI, or successfully appealed to portions of the Islamic world for support, or kept an invasion on hold by surrendering a few low-level al-Qaeda fighters and offering protracted negotiations.

Although we were later told that General Franks had indeed recommended to the president and the secretary of defense that the United States go into Afghanistan with three divisions (President Bush and Secretary Rumsfeld immediately rejected the idea), we took comfort from one piece of information making the rounds of the Washington grapevine: the president wanted action *now*. In turn, we knew that he would not be willing to wait the months necessary to move and position a force that size into Afghanistan. As September drifted into October, we knew that U.S. naval forces were moving to the Arabian Sea, which meant strike aircraft from U.S. aircraft carriers and U.S. Marines would be available to Central Command. U.S. military aircraft began deploying to the Persian Gulf, and a one-thousand-man force of the 10th Mountain Division was designated for dispatch to Uzbekistan, presumably to guard the air bases there. We assumed that U.S. satellites were examining every possible inch of Afghanistan and U.S. special operations forces probably were in bases in Uzbekistan, Tajikistan, and Pakistan and entering Afghanistan to conduct reconnaissance and talk to locals. Still, we figured it would be a few weeks before any force that would have any chance of success in Afghanistan would be ready.

THE AIR CAMPAIGN

When the air strikes began on Sunday, October 7, 2001, we were pleased. The necessary blow was being struck—swiftly and surely— on a schedule even better than we had hoped.

The air campaign began with strikes by cruise missiles fired from U.S. Navy warships; heavy bombers flying from the "unsinkable aircraft carrier," the island of Diego Garcia; and U.S. Navy strike aircraft from U.S. aircraft carriers. Two days later, the air strikes began in broad daylight; on October 11, the initial target list was complete. The bombing had destroyed the Afghan air-defense missile system, the remnants of the Afghan air force, heavy equipment (such as tanks), and the Afghan telephone system. The Taliban now had no way of knocking down U.S. aircraft except by handheld antiaircraft missiles, antiaircraft artillery, and machine guns and little left in the way to counter lighter ground forces. The demise of the telephone system forced the Taliban and al-Qaeda to use radio and cellular telephones for communication—both of which were susceptible to interception, jamming, and surveillance. After the initial list of targets was hit, coalition air power ranged everywhere over Afghanistan, chasing the Taliban and dismantling other parts of the Taliban's military power—in other words, preparing the battlefield for the ground offensive to come.

One problem with the air campaign, however, was its desultory pace. Certainly, the coalition aircraft were hitting their targets, but for the first couple of weeks, the aircraft were restricted to those that came "from the sea" from U.S. aircraft carriers in the Arabian Sea and the Gulf of Oman, from U.S. Air Force heavy bombers (B-52s and B-1s) from Diego Garcia, and on occasion from B-2 "Spirit" bombers flying round trips from their bases in Missouri to Afghanistan and back without landing. Moreover, almost every aircraft involved needed aerial refueling support, and this significantly stressed our tanker force, which is moving into bloc obsolescence. It was clear that there was a compelling need to modernize our aerial tanker force.

In Operation Enduring Freedom, General Franks chose to use advanced communications technology to exercise his command from the headquarters of U.S. Central Command at MacDill Air Force Base in Tampa, Florida. As "gee-whiz" as that was, separating a theater commander, especially one who is expected to exercise day-to-day *command*, not just provide general guidance, from the forces he is supposed to command is asking for trouble. So it turned out to be in Operation Enduring Freedom. During the air campaign, Central Command often refused to delegate decisions about hitting targets; all questions about whether or not to strike at a target were referred back to Central Command. This disrupted what the Air Force refers to as "time critical targeting," in which a target of opportunity presents itself and there is limited time to act on it. Too often during the air campaign, there were targets that could have—and should have—been struck, but the authorization to do so was not immediately available. Often, too, the rules of engagement were too restrictive, and because of them, opportunities were lost.

There were at least two "opportunities lost" to hit the leader of the Taliban, Mullah Omar. On the first night of the war, a CIA-controlled armed Predator unmanned aerial vehicle, armed with two Hellfire antitank missiles, spotted a convoy in which Mullah Omar was said to be traveling. It would have been simple for the UAV operator to fire the missiles at the convoy and perhaps kill the top man in the Taliban. The rules of engagement for the CIA, however, were such that the operator had to ask for permission to fire. The aerial images and permission request were forwarded to U.S. Central Command; there, a *military lawyer* made the decision *not* to fire.

Another time, Mullah Omar was tracked to a building in Afghanistan. A strike package was hastily put together to hit the target. But an analyst—looking at the images streaming in from the UAV circling the building—spotted a tall, cylindrical structure nearby. Was it a minaret or a chimney or something else? The rules of engagement forbid the deliberate targeting of mosques. While those looking at the streaming video from the image tried to figure out if the building was a mosque or a factory, Mullah Omar made his escape. There should have been some clear delegation of authority *downward*, some recognition that "trigger-pullers" need an immediate response on manhunts, and that the answers as cleared by bureaucrats and lawyers aren't always the best ones.

Another problem with the initial air campaign was that it was somewhat misdirected. The destruction of the Taliban's air defenses and communications facilities made sense, but afterward, the need to pummel other fixed, preselected targets seemed less pressing. When someone remarked that the U.S. aerial campaign was an attempt to bomb the Taliban back into the Stone Age, Paul retorted by saying, "They are already *in* the Stone Age." The serious point to be made was that the air campaign should have been quickly redirected to destroying military units rather than fixed sites. The combined forces air component commander (CFACC) wanted a far more aggressive air campaign but was restricted initially by the CENTCOM staff.

THE COLLAPSE OF THE TALIBAN

Why did the widely feared Taliban collapse so quickly in the fall of 2001, so quickly in fact that in less than two months, it was driven out of its cultural capital of Kandahar and over the border to Pakistan? The answer is coordinated American firepower delivered from the air and on the ground. Both elements were crucial. The Clinton administration had made a habit of relying purely on symbolic air strikes when it wanted to deploy military power. But to win an objective it takes more than air strikes, it takes soldiers on the ground. And Operation Enduring Freedom as it was actually employed got the balance exactly right, using American and indigenous forces, including rapidly deployable units—Special Forces and Marines—U.S. airpower (lots of it), and the Afghan Northern Alliance.

The U.S. Army's Special Forces—popularly known as the "Green Berets"—have long had the mission of raising, training, and leading indigenous forces. In Southeast Asia, they organized the mountain tribes of Vietnam's Central Highlands, "the Montagnards," into special operations forces to battle units of the North Vietnamese Army and the Viet Cong. In Afghanistan, the Green Berets, and their colleagues in the CIA, prepared the Northern Alliance for a far grander job—liberating their entire country. It worked because of U.S. airpower. The Special Forces acted as the "eyes" of that airpower, using advanced targeting technology, such as laser designators, that could guide precision weapons, or "smart bombs," to targets. The Special Forces' presence also indicated that the Americans were *committed* to the defeat of the Taliban and al-Qaeda and that we shared a common combat bond with the Afghans.

On September 11, 2001, the Northern Alliance held only 10 percent of the country. By October 20, 2001, three U.S. Special Forces "A-teams" had entered Afghanistan—their paths prepared and their welcomes arranged by CIA agents—and were in contact with the Northern Alliance commanders (two A-teams were inserted around Mazar-i-Sharif; another was with Northern Alliance forces near Kabul). In one week's time, the Green Berets had honed the skills of Alliance soldiers, demonstrated to them the usefulness of their targeting equipment, and used it to bring "smart bombs" onto Taliban positions (as well as some "dumb" ones from B-52s). The effect of the heavy bombing was devastating to the Taliban defenders. So impressed were they with the ability of the Americans to put bombs apparently anywhere they wished that the Taliban referred to U.S. targeting equipment, the laser designators especially, as "the death ray." The combination of accurate, heavy bombing and a motivated ground force was sufficient to drive the Taliban out of Mazar-i-Sharif on November 9, 2001. For the forces around Kabul, the combination worked its magic as well: by November 12, Northern Alliance forces had entered Kabul (as well as captured two other important cities in the western and northeastern parts of Afghanistan). Two days later, the Taliban had fled the capital, retreating toward the Afghanistan-Pakistan border or toward the city of Kandahar.

In mid-November, a Green Beret A-team joined up with the Pushtun leader Hamid Karzai (now Afghanistan's president) in the southern part of Afghanistan near the city of Kandahar. On November 25, after a bold movement in which they leapfrogged from amphibious

ships in the Arabian Sea to Pakistani airfields and thence to an abandoned airfield south of Kandahar, several hundred U.S. Marines
entered the battle. After establishing their camp, they fanned out
searching for Taliban, al-Qaeda, and weapons dumps. On December
6, the city of Kandahar fell to Pushtun fighters recruited by Karzai and
supported by the Green Berets and U.S. airpower. Thus, in two
months, the Taliban and al-Qaeda were driven out of every major city
in Afghanistan.

This victory could have been achieved sooner if Central Command
had listened to its component commanders in the area of operations
and attacked the Taliban and al-Qaeda forces occupying these cities
within the first week of the campaign. This would have shortened the
campaign significantly. Unfortunately, the Special Forces A-teams
were not inserted prior to the beginning of hostilities and General
Franks' staff was conducting a classic campaign versus a modern campaign of blitz warfare.

SECURING THE VICTORY?

As broadly satisfying as these victories in Afghanistan were, there was
still work to do, especially in the areas along the Pakistan-Afghanistan
border. Intelligence—and rumor—indicated that the surviving
"Arabs," meaning Osama bin Laden and other members of al-Qaeda,
had gone to ground in a complex of caves in the Tora Bora mountains
in eastern Afghanistan. U.S. Central Command decided to mount an
operation to dig these al-Qaeda fighters out of the caves, killing or capturing them.

When it came to capturing Osama bin Laden and his terrorists, Central Command made a mistake. Instead of using the one thousand men
of the 10th Mountain Division or redirecting the Marines in
Afghanistan onto the mission, General Franks decided to apply the
same formula in this fight that had been so successful in other places
in Afghanistan: Afghan fighters backed by U.S. Special Forces and

supported by U.S. airpower. For a blocking force, Central Command depended on Pakistani border units, not American ones. While the Tora Bora battles undoubtedly led to the deaths of hundreds of al-Qaeda terrorists, the "big fish"—to include Osama bin Laden—escaped. With so much at stake, the blocking force straddling the Afghanistan-Pakistan border should have been an American or mixed coalition force; that way, General Franks would have been sure that a strong effort was made to shut the back door out of Afghanistan and trap as many al-Qaeda as possible between two forces

Beginning in March 2002, Operation Anaconda was the last "main force" action of Operation Enduring Freedom and the first one to use large numbers of more "conventional" soldiers—the 10th Mountain Division and the 101st Airborne (Air Assault) Division as well as a broad variety of special operations forces, drawn from different countries. While we were glad to see some of the U.S. Army's larger units involved in the fight in Afghanistan, there was considerable "friction" between the Army and the Air Force during this bold winter offensive against al-Qaeda enclaves. There were also some hairy moments when a few of the landing zones for airmobile assaults ended up being right under the noses of al-Qaeda and Taliban fighters. This was caused by lack of coordination between the 10th Mountain Division commander with the CFACC. Fortunately, the lessons learned during Anaconda were applied in Operation Iraqi Freedom with great success.

Although we had some objections to the initial plans and the conduct of the final phases of the campaign, we agreed that, overall, Operation Enduring Freedom had been a huge success. The Taliban had been broken and al-Qaeda routed. The president and his national security team had demonstrated strength and resolve. And the U.S. military had executed an extraordinarily swift and effective strike from an extraordinary distance and shown far more creative thinking than it is usually given credit for.

With Operation Enduring Freedom, special operations forces had truly entered into a new era, combining their traditional missions with a new one of acting as the "eyes-on-the-ground" for precision air-power. The Navy proved that though the battlefield was landlocked and many hundreds of miles from any ocean, our aircraft carriers and their embarked aircraft could be a crucial component of the air campaign in Afghanistan. The Navy flew more than 70 percent of all combat sorties. Yet, thanks to the participation of the Air Force's heavy bomber fleet in the air campaign, the Air Force dropped 80 percent of the bombs used. The B-1s, B-2s, and B-52s were capable of dropping up to twenty-four precision-guided bombs per aircraft. While we could have used more aerial refueling aircraft, another aerial improvement was the introduction of various unmanned aerial vehicles that provided unparalleled aerial reconnaissance. And the effectiveness of America's "boots on the ground" trigger-pullers—Army, Navy SEALs, and Marines—showed what a few good men can truly do. Watching our victory in Afghanistan was a proud and glorious experience, but we knew that this was only the beginning.

CHAPTER FIVE

NOTES FROM A CAMPAIGN OF LIBERATION: IRAQ

AFTER THE SUCCESS OF Operation Enduring Freedom in Afghanistan, some analysts suggested that with al-Qaeda effectively scattered, the United States should return to the law enforcement paradigm of counterterrorism. Others insisted that the United States should follow its victory in Afghanistan with an effort to bring peace between the Israelis and the Palestinians, or between India and Pakistan. But we knew these strategies wouldn't work; they were the outdated strategies of previous administrations. For eight years, the Clinton administration treated terrorism as a law-enforcement matter and focused on the "peace process" in the Middle East. During those same eight years, al-Qaeda gained in strength and audacity, escalating its attacks on American targets until the events of September 11. Based on experience, that is no model for preventing and defeating terrorism.

On February 22, 2002, we left the Washington, D.C., studios of FOX News Channel for a working lunch at the restaurant La Colline, during which we sketched out the campaign against our next selected target in the war on terror: Saddam Hussein. Why did we think Saddam Hussein should be next? Saddam Hussein compared himself to the medieval Muslim hero Saladin—ironically, a Kurd—and his ambitions ran to the creation of a "Greater Iraq" that would gobble up large portions of Iraq's neighbors or, as in the case of Kuwait, swallow them whole and become the dominant power in the Middle East. To that end, he invaded Iran in 1980, and fought the Iranians for eight years. He invaded Kuwait in 1990. It was after his ouster from Kuwait that we discovered just how far advanced was his effort to build a nuclear bomb.

In the aftermath of the 1991 Gulf War, international inspectors dismantled Saddam Hussein's chemical, biological, and nuclear weapons programs, but the trained personnel necessary for reconstituting those weapons remained, as did Saddam Hussein's ambitions to build these weapons and, based on his insatiable desire for cash, become a proliferator of weapons of mass destruction.

Saddam Hussein's Iraq kept bad company—as one might expect of a regime that practiced mass executions, torture, and arbitrary arrest and imprisonment and used chemical weapons against its own people. Iraq had extensive dealings with terrorists. Two Palestinians at the top of many terrorism-related "most wanted" lists in the 1980s and the 1990s—Abu Nidal (real name: Sabri al-Banna) and Abu Abbas—were given sanctuary by Saddam Hussein. Abu Nidal led an organization that committed a number of bloody attacks in Europe, the Middle East, and South Asia. Abu Abbas masterminded the 1985 hijacking of the cruise ship the *Achille Lauro,* a crime that included the murder of a wheelchair-bound American passenger. Iraq provided training camps for terrorists, most notoriously at Salman Pak, south of Baghdad, where an obsolescent Boeing 707 was used to train terrorists to hijack airliners. Iraq made cash payments to the families of Palestinian suicide bombers. Saddam Hussein's vice president, Taha Yasin Ramadan, was specifically tasked with supporting the terrorist activities of the PLO, Hamas, and Palestinian Islamic Jihad. The Iraqis had tried to assassinate President George H. W. Bush. Iraq had ties to al-Qaeda, as was reported by both Sudanese and Czechoslovakian intelligence. In addition, the al-Qaeda affiliate, Ansar al-Islam, was based in northern Iraq, where it was a potentially destabilizing influence on Kurdish opposition groups.

Saddam Hussein's combined sins of massive human rights viola-tions, state support of international terrorism, and development and use of weapons of mass destruction made his removal our first prior-ity after Operation Enduring Freedom. Some people suggested that the best option vis-à-vis Iraq was to continue the de facto containment policy of the 1990s. We rejected that idea for a number of reasons. First, Iraq had subverted the sanctions through illegal means with the cooperation of regimes like Syria. Second, international support for maintaining the sanctions was wavering. Third, we knew that French, German, and Russian businesses continued to fuel Saddam Hussein's illegal weapons programs. There was every reason to believe that Sad-dam Hussein would develop—or had already stockpiled—weapons of mass destruction; every intelligence agency in the world agreed on that point. And it was reasonable to believe, especially given the Iraqi attempt to assassinate former president George H. W. Bush, that Sad-dam Hussein might provide such weapons, covertly and with plausi-ble deniability, to a terrorist organization to strike the United States. After September 11, 2001, we weren't willing to take that risk.

A few days earlier, Tom had appeared on FOX News Channel's *Special Report with Brit Hume* with Dennis Ross, former special ambassador to the Middle East during both the Bush and Clinton administrations. After the show, he asked Ambassador Ross what sig-nificance a "lightning campaign" that brought down Saddam Hussein in less than thirty days would have politically. Ambassador Ross replied that since most Arab governments held Saddam Hussein in utter contempt, the only potential source of objection would be the suffering of the Iraqi people if the campaign dragged out into a slugfest lasting for months. If the United States could topple Saddam Hussein in less than thirty days, he said, the reaction of Arab governments would be limited to muted pro forma objections.

After we had counted off the reasons for getting rid of Saddam Hus-sein, therefore, Tom's first question to Paul was "Could the Army exe-cute a thirty-day ground campaign?" Almost immediately, Paul replied in the affirmative. We then got to work on the general outlines of the campaign, "a war of liberation," using a paper napkin to do so.

The center of gravity of the regime was not the Iraqi army but the government in Baghdad. In our plan, therefore, allied forces would drive to Baghdad from three directions—the north, west, and south, with possible jumping off points in Turkey, Saudi Arabia (or possibly Jordan), and Kuwait. We agreed that with the right tactics and techniques, victory could be achieved in less than thirty days, with a force smaller than that used in the 1991 Gulf War (we estimated that eleven or twelve brigades or 100,000-plus U.S. troops—not counting coalition and Iraqi opposition forces—could do the job), and with relatively few allied and Iraqi casualties.

The important element in this campaign would be the manner of its execution. For that, we embraced the concept of "blitz warfare"—a simultaneous and ferocious assault by air power and fast-moving conventional ground forces and special operations forces—all married to the most advanced information technology. Since we conceived this campaign as one of liberation, Iraqi freedom fighters were an important element of the force. Based on our conversations with members of the Iraqi National Congress and high-ranking Iraqi exiles, we estimated that as many as ten thousand Iraqis could be recruited and trained in time for the campaign.

THE THIRTY-DAY TAKEDOWN

We knew the oil fields had to be seized early to avoid an environmental catastrophe like the one Iraq attempted to create in Kuwait in 1991 and to ensure that the new government of Iraq would have sufficient economic resources. Likewise, neutralizing any Iraqi missile threat was a top priority. The major objectives, however, were to isolate and decapitate the regime's command and control and knock out the regime's underpinnings by defeating in detail the military and security units that kept Saddam Hussein's regime secure in its position of power. The Iraqi army did not, in our estimate, need to be destroyed entirely. Defeat the regime's command and control, we thought, defeat those units most loyal to Saddam Hussein, and the remaining Iraqi conscripts would fade away rather than fight for their oppressor.

As we sketched out the plan's outline, we were mindful of its logistical demands, and we factored in shifts required by politics, domestic and international. After a couple of weeks of discussing and adjusting the details of the plan, we mentioned it to Bill O'Reilly at the FOX News Channel party before the annual TV and Radio Banquet in Washington, D.C. After we laid out for him our "War of Liberation" strategy in very broad terms, he booked us for the next evening's show. We knew appearing on *The O'Reilly Factor* to discuss the plan was something of a risk. In the past, we had acted solely as military *analysts*. Presenting our plan came close to *advocacy*. But having stuck our necks out on Bill's show, we did it again the following week, when Paul appeared on *FOX and Friends* promoting the idea of a "war of liberation" that could be won in thirty days.

Both of us have worked with the Pentagon and the Congress, and we knew our plan would receive a mixed reaction. Pentagon planners and members of Congress were relatively cautious. Some "think tank" critics thought we were overselling the capabilities of our armed forces. Their caution, their doubts didn't sway us. Throughout the rest of the winter and well into the summer and fall of 2002, we promoted a "war of liberation" that could be achieved through the application of "blitz warfare." Tom did so in print in an op-ed in the *Wall Street Journal* and in testimony to both the Senate Armed Services Committee and Senate Foreign Relations Committee. We did so as well, in numerous meetings in Washington, D.C., and during our appearances on FOX News Channel. We knew we were making headway. Eventually, the words "War of Liberation" began filtering out in press conferences and materials from the Department of Defense, the State Department, and the White House. By the time Congress reconvened in September 2002, members of the Department of Defense were asking us for practical details of our plan and inquiring as to how we had come by our estimates of Iraqi morale and other factors.

When we asked why the Pentagon—the paid experts who were drawing up the real plans—was asking us, retired generals, for the details of *our* plan, we were told that, insofar as a campaign against Iraq was concerned, the Pentagon had initially envisaged "Desert Storm II," a massive operation with as many as *eight divisions and 500,000 troops.* After Operation Enduring Freedom, however, Secretary Rumsfeld, General Franks, and other leaders in the Defense Department had come to believe that a smaller joint force backed by air power and supported by special operations forces could liberate Iraq. So we confirmed two things: first, that the Pentagon was planning the liberation of Iraq; and second, that our message resonated within the upper echelons of the Defense Department.

We were surprised at how many liberal commentators and Democratic politicians opposed the liberation of Iraq. We had assumed there was bipartisan agreement on this point. After all, President Clinton had ordered strikes against some of Saddam Hussein's facilities for building and storing weapons of mass destruction in Operation Desert Fox in 1998, without United Nations approval. In 1998, Congress had passed the Iraqi Liberation Act by an overwhelming majority, which made "regime change" in Iraq the official policy of the United States. Still, we heard many fervent arguments against the liberation of Iraq among them:

"The liberation of Iraq will overstretch the American military."

While it was true the U.S. military was conducting operations at a tempo unmatched since the 1991 Persian Gulf War, deploying four to five infantry divisions and a reinforced Marine Expeditionary Force plus air and naval forces—a combined operations total of roughly 250,000 troops—to Iraq would not overstretch a military that had more than a million in active-duty personnel.

"The liberation of Iraq will distract us from the war on terror."

There were two ill-founded ideas behind this objection. The first stemmed from a narrow definition of terrorism—that is, outside al-Qaeda there is no terrorism. It is true that Saddam Hussein was not as active in supporting terrorists as Iran and Libya, but he was still a blatant state sponsor of terror, and knocking him over was not a diversion from the fight against the Web of Terror, but an integral part of it, especially since his defeat would deny terrorists one source of weapons of mass destruction. The second wrong idea was that the United States couldn't chew gum and walk at the same time: that is, we couldn't fight al-Qaeda and Iraq at the same time. The fact is, we could and we did.

"Iraq will use chemical and biological weapons against our forces."

We could never quite understand why this was supposed to be a "showstopper." Admittedly, operating in a chemical or biological environment is at once cumbersome and dangerous. However, that is why the U.S. military has put so much money into countermeasures—from chemical warfare suits for soldiers to filtration systems for vehicles—as well as chemical and biological reconnaissance capabilities. Moreover, chemical and biological weapons are "equal opportunity" weapons; an attack using, say, mustard gas can harm the forces that use the weapon; all it takes is a shift in wind. We were confident that given the state of the Iraqi army in late 2002, if Iraq used these weapons they might prove to be more dangerous to the Iraqi army than to ours.

"Baghgrad."

Another argument against the liberation of Iraq was that even if the campaign were initially successful in defeating the Iraqi army, it would bog down in the streets of the Iraqi capital. The Special Republican Guard and other forces would turn Baghdad into an updated version of Stalingrad, a bloody house-by-house battle that would cause thousands of American casualties and tens of thousands of Iraqi casualties and might even lead to the defeat of the U.S. forces. This was a legitimate concern—and the very reason why we stressed the need to adopt a plan for a swift campaign using overwhelming firepower and focused on toppling the regime. We also had human intelligence that no fortifications were being built in Baghdad; the Republican Guards were not training for urban warfare; and no Republican Guard divisions were being allowed into Baghdad (because Saddam Hussein feared they might launch a coup). Finally, if there had been a siege of Baghdad, American tactics would have made it a very different scenario than what happened at Stalingrad. We were confident that house-to-house fighting would not be necessary to win such a battle. Our confidence stemmed from our knowledge that the combined forces air component commander (CFACC) had been developed and trained for "urban close air support" at Nellis Air Force Base. Centered on the use of precision munitions striking at regime targets, it would have broken the back of any major, organized resistance and prevented the nightmarish "Baghgrad" scenario from happening.

Civilian Casualties.

Every war kills people who are not in uniform. But we argued—and Afghanistan showed—that joint operations that combine precision guided weaponry and special operations forces, while not perfectly safe, minimize civilian casualties—more so than ever before. The campaign we planned was designed to shield civilians by achieving quick results and by focusing on the regime that held the Iraqi people captive to a ruthless tyrant, rather than waging a massive "total war." Again, based on the experience in Operation Enduring Freedom, we knew that every possible safeguard to prevent civilian casualties would be in place. The risk of civilian casualties was more than outweighed by the reward of a successful campaign: freeing the Iraqi people from a dictator whose deliberately and systematically conducted mass executions of his political opponents, real and perceived. In the end, the moral calculus favored action against Saddam Hussein. All postwar polls show that the Iraqi people hold the same view.

"The Recruiting Sergeant for Terrorism."

Opponents of the war predicted the Iraq campaign would drive more young men into the ranks of terrorist organizations. Our response was that the campaign might lead to a short-term spurt of public support for Saddam Hussein, but that not many young men would be motivated to join an Islamic terrorist group in order to avenge a disgraced dictator whose appeal was not to radical Islamism, but to Arab nationalism, an ideology held in contempt by many radical Islamists. And which is the better recruiter—the Ba'ath Party successfully thumbing its nose at the United States, or Saddam Hussein captured or dead, his mass graves and corruption exposed, and Iraqis cheering their liberation?

The Arab Street.

This mythical beast haunts the dreams and waking thoughts of many responsible journalists, editorialists, legislators, academics, and government officials. When angered, it is, allegedly, a fearsome creature, lashing out indiscriminately, wreaking havoc, and devouring whole governments. Of course what the "Arab street" really amounts to is footage for the nightly news—and no more than that.

Free Iraqi Forces.

Another thing that perplexed us, aside from liberal and Democratic opposition to liberating Iraq, was the inattention of the administration to Iraqi resistance organizations, including the Iraqi National Congress. The State Department, CIA, and Defense Department all had their various reasons and excuses for not dealing with or adequately supporting the Iraqi exiles, but we found these excuses unconvincing.

We say this while well knowing the dangers of émigré organizations. Often they can be much more effective at soliciting money from the U.S. government than achieving any results in their home country. Another danger is that these organizations can be fronts for or penetrated by spies.

When Paul accepted an invitation to meet with the head of the Washington office of the Iraqi National Congress, Entifadh Qanbar, a former Iraqi air force captain, he was directed to an address not on K Street or Connecticut Avenue or any other high-priced location, but approximately ten blocks from the Capitol, off Pennsylvania Avenue, Southeast. There, Paul found a two-story row house, unmarked with any sign indicating the INC's presence. Mr. Qanbar explained that it was from this house that he and his small staff ran the INC's entire U.S. effort. This was an organization that preferred doing hard work to luxuriating in plush offices.

The INC Washington staff gathered information on the Iraqi government—largely from American-based Iraqi defectors with relatives still living in Iraq—and passed it on to the INC's London headquarters for analysis. At the INC's London office, analysts combined that information with the information that the INC received from sources in the Middle East (including some brave agents operating in Iraq) and Europe. They, in turn, sent the combined analyzed intelligence to Mr. Qanbar, who passed it on to his contacts in the U.S. Defense Intelligence Agency.

Mr. Qanbar told Paul that though the INC had a lead role in pushing the Iraq Liberation Act through Congress—which had made regime change the official policy of the U.S. government—the INC had received only $5 million of a promised $97 million from a grudging State Department and CIA. The Pentagon, however, had proved friendlier, and it was through the Department of Defense that he had established decent ties with the Defense Intelligence Agency.

Mr. Qanbar took Paul down the street to a second house that served as the repository of information on the Iraqi regime, including its military, intelligence service, and internal security organizations, which the INC had worked into an exceptionally detailed order-of-battle. There were also organizational charts and lists of Iraqi officers and civil servants, complete with their assignments, addresses, and telephone numbers, as well as, in many cases, their cellular telephone numbers and their e-mail addresses. The files were extensive, up-to-date, and, from what we knew of the Iraqi military from other sources, accurate.

What made the INC even more impressive to Paul was that Mr. Qanbar made no exaggerated claims for the INC or for the information it had gathered. In fact, Mr. Qanbar said that the INC was frustrated by what it still *didn't know* about the regime. The INC had no reliable source in the upper echelon of the Ba'ath Party or Iraqi intelligence and, although some of the more recent defectors were men of high rank, Saddam Hussein's fetish for security meant that they brought out little information of lasting value on the higher levels of the Iraqi government. Another gap the INC admitted to concerned Iraq's weapons of mass destruction; there was little recent information on the location of any weapons and the status of the programs.

Why did this make the INC more credible? Look at it this way. The information that was most prized by the coalition in the run-up to the campaign against Saddam Hussein was information about the upper echelon of the Iraqi government and Iraq's WMD programs. If the INC had wanted to garner attention and money from the U.S. government, it could have touted its information as the final word on these topics and hinted that, yes, it had highly placed sources in the Iraqi WMD program and at the very top of the Iraqi government. The INC chose not to make those claims, because they were not true.

During the next few months, our contacts with the INC grew stronger. Not long after Paul's meeting with Mr. Qanbar, the INC invited Tom to meet the staff and look at the information that the INC had on file. He came away impressed not only by what he had read, but also by the overall tone of the operation.

During the next few months, our opinion of the INC became even more positive. The information they provided to us compared favorably with that we received from other sources. We became aware of just how extensive their networks were, reaching across the United States, Europe, and the Middle East. Through the INC, we met many high-level defectors from Ba'athist Iraq—including Khidir Hamza, a nuclear scientist widely known as "Saddam's Bomb-maker." He gave us excellent insight into the situation in Iraq and allowed us to set new information we had gathered into proper perspective. The INC's sources, leaders, and staff members struck us as well educated, well informed, and sincerely committed to the overthrow of the Ba'athist regime and the establishment of a democratic state in its stead. They were also mindful of the work that would be necessary to carry out both these aims.

Just as important as this information, however, was the INC's willingness to serve in Operation Iraqi Freedom. Its members wanted to help the allied coalition forces by offering intelligence and information that only an Iraqi national would know. Almost from the beginning of our relationship, the INC told us that they had no shortage of volunteers who would accompany our forces into the field, and help with everything from acting as translators to assisting with psychological operations.

We tried to interest administration officials in taking up the INC's offers of assistance. Tom recommended that a senior Iraqi general who was working with the INC, General Najeb al Salhi, be attached to U.S. Central Command as an advisor. We also recommended that small teams of trained Iraqi émigrés (drawn from all legitimate groups) be attached to frontline battalions and companies. The members of these teams would act as interpreters, translators, and guides; aid in intelligence work and prisoner interrogation; help with psychological and information operations; and serve as the point of contact with local Iraqis. After hostilities ended, these volunteers would be invaluable to any civil affairs effort.

Our suggestions and others for using the Iraqi émigrés went for naught, however, until late 2002, when Secretary Rumsfeld took the INC completely under the wing of the Defense Department. He ordered a program to recruit and train Iraqi volunteers. Approximately three thousand Iraqis were eventually recruited, assembled at an air base in Hungary, and formed into the Free Iraqi Forces (FIF). Unfortunately, the majority of these forces were not used and their talents, their language skills, and their local area knowledge were not taken advantage of by Central Command's planners. This was a major mistake.

Although the Pentagon finally came around to the need to utilize the INC and the FIF, the effort proved to be ultimately disappointing. Entifadh Qanbar was eventually assigned to the U.S. Central Command headquarters. In late March, U.S. C-130s flew six hundred of the Free Iraq Forces to an air base near An Nasiriyah and, from there, they hooked up with U.S. units headed toward Baghdad. They performed well, but had the Pentagon created a larger force earlier (like the 10,000-member force we had suggested) and placed them with the coalition forces well *before* the invasion of Iraq began, they would have been much more effective.

The 4th Infantry Division.

The 4th Infantry Division was another underutilized asset. It has performed magnificently in the counterinsurgency war in Iraq, its crowning achievement being the capture of Saddam Hussein in December 2003. Few might remember it now, but immediately before Operation Iraqi Freedom, it was doubtful that this unit of 17,000 soldiers would even participate in the campaign.

Dubbed the "Digital Division," the 4th Infantry Division has a place of pride in the Army as its most technologically advanced fighting unit. Under the plan the Pentagon drew up, ships carrying the 4th Infantry Division's equipment would have landed in Turkey, the unit's soldiers, who had flown ahead to meet the ships, then would have unloaded their equipment, and the division then would have moved overland through Turkey and the Kurd-held areas in northern Iraq before driving south toward Baghdad. It was to be the anvil for the forces driving up from the south led by the 3rd ID. This would have enabled the coalition forces to defeat the Iraqi forces in about twelve to fourteen days. But it was not to be.

In January 2003, however, the Turkish parliament—under an arcane parliamentary rule—rejected the landing and the transit of the 4th Infantry Division. With the 4th Infantry Division effectively withdrawn from the order-of-battle, U.S. Central Command now had no way to cut the Damascus-Baghdad road, a route taken by jihadists, arms smugglers, and, as we were later informed by reliable sources, Iraqi weapons of mass destruction on their way to be hidden in Syria and the Bekaa Valley, where we believe they are now.

Without the 4th Infantry Division driving down from Turkey, U.S. commanders were limited to deploying special operations forces and whatever Kurdish forces they could muster to move south toward Mosul and Kirkuk and to the west near Syria. The problem was that their mobility would be limited and they could not bring much firepower to bear beyond that which coalition airpower provided. Thus, Saddam Hussein would have been free to move forces to the south to face the deep penetration attacks of the Army and Marines.

It has been widely reported—for example, by Oliver North in his excellent book on the campaign, *War Stories: Operation Iraqi Freedom*—that General Tommy Franks, the head of Central Command, decided to use the 4th Infantry Division as a strategic deception. He did not order the ships carrying the division's equipment to rush through the Suez Canal and around to the Persian Gulf. Instead, he held the ships off the Turkish coast, giving the Iraqi army the impression that a secret deal was in the works to deploy the 4th Infantry Division to the northern front. Apparently, this ruse worked and some of Saddam Hussein's army held their positions north of Baghdad until it was too late to attempt to save the regime. However, they never had a chance from the very beginning against this magnificent combined air, land, and sea force.

Central Command eventually did open up a "northern front" with the 173rd Airborne Brigade. After linking with the special operations forces and Kurdish forces in the area, the Brigade moved southward toward Mosul, Kirkuk, and other cities in the northern region and essentially was a fixing force, as it was too light to be decisive.

Initially, it could have been different. When we put forth the plan for war of liberation, we suggested a force coming into northern Iraq via the Kurdish areas and Turkey. We did not, however, envision a force as heavy or as large as the 4th Infantry Division doing that particular job, but rather a lighter force such as a brigade of the 101st Airborne Division using indigenous Iraqi forces such as the Kurds. This force would have had a smaller footprint in Turkey and yet would have packed more punch and mobility than the 173rd Brigade's paratroopers.

It still perplexes us that, knowing the political situation in Turkey, the Bush administration did not try to move a smaller, lighter force through Turkey rather than the almost 80,000-strong force proposed. Without question this large force would have achieved the swift decisive results that General Franks desired. However, given Turkey's enduring stand against terrorism, the Turkish prime minister and his cabinet might have approved the passage of a smaller unit, much as Jordan apparently allowed special operations forces to carry out their work from airfields in that country. In any case, the flexibility exhibited by General Franks's forces was extraordinary.

THE REAL TAKEDOWN:
OPERATION IRAQI FREEDOM

Operation Iraqi Freedom was a resounding victory for the coalition and an amazing achievement of American arms. As we write this chapter, we are fast approaching the campaign's first anniversary and, with the dust raised by the campaign now all but settled, it seems a good time to evaluate it in order to determine what it demonstrated about how we will fight in the twenty-first century.

No Sanctuaries:

Like Operation Enduring Freedom, the campaign in Iraq stakes out an important grand strategic principle: if you are part of the Web of Terror, if you sponsor, support, and conduct terrorism or pursue weapons of mass destruction, count yourself part of the Axis of Evil, and the United States and its allies will reserve the option of taking you out.

Actionable Intelligence:

For commanders at any level, actionable intelligence is, to borrow a term, "news you can use." While background information about, say, the personality of an air force commander certainly is interesting and can be useful, it is not as valuable as determining how that same commander plans to fight the air battle, the disposition of his forces, or the presence of any new weapons system.

Thanks to the efforts of the CIA, special operations forces, and the Iraqi National Congress, there was no shortage of actionable intelligence and it was of exceptionally high quality, helping the allied forces to keep Saddam Hussein's regime off-balance throughout Operation Iraqi Freedom. In Operation Iraqi Freedom, the integration of military special operations forces and the clandestine services of the Central Intelligence Agency was a marked success. We should build and improve on that success.

Special Operations:

The performance of special operations forces in Iraq confirmed the lesson we had learned in Afghanistan: special operations forces have entered a new era. In the past, most policymakers and high-ranking officers considered special operations forces useful only for such tasks as reconnaissance, raiding, surveillance, and hostage rescue. Their high profile and relatively lavish financial resources made them objects of resentment by many in the military who often derided them as "snake eaters" whose machismo (and financial resources) was in inverse proportion to their usefulness on the battlefield.

Improvements in technology related to communications and targeting gave special operations forces the ability to work closely with U.S. air power, using precision munitions, at the tactical and strategic level. In turn, that "marriage" of technology, highly trained personnel, and firepower gives these forces a striking power and presence on the battlefield that is hugely disproportionate to their numbers.

This does not mean that the special operations forces have abandoned their more traditional roles. Leapfrogging out of Kurdish-held areas in Iraq and bases in Kuwait and Jordan, coalition special operations forces established bases in western Iraq (bases that were known as H-1, H-2, and H-3) and from there went on to deploy via special operations helicopters and transport aircraft like MH-47s, MH-53s, and MC-130s, to conduct raiding and reconnaissance missions. Special operations forces seized the Iraqi oil fields, preserving them from sabotage, as well as many of the river crossings that were vital to the rapid coalition advance toward Baghdad.

Based on their performance in Afghanistan and Iraq, Secretary Rumsfeld's commitment to improving and expanding U.S. special operations capabilities is absolutely justified. Any military spending that sharpens the sword, rather than extending the tail of noncombat forces, is money well spent.

Above It All—Coalition Airpower:

The story of airpower in Operation Iraqi Freedom can be summed up in two words—*precision* and *lethality*. We remember how awestruck some reporters were about the use of precision weapons by U.S. warplanes in the 1991 Gulf War. Often lost in the gee-whiz journalism about cruise missiles and laser-guided bombs was the fact that only about 13 percent of the aerial bombs used in that war were precision-guided weapons. In Operation Iraqi Freedom, almost 70 percent of all munitions used by U.S. airpower were precision-guided weapons, a five-fold increase. Moreover, all strike aircraft in the U.S. inventory—to include the B-1s, B-2s, and B-52s of the U.S. heavy-bomber force—now are capable of using these precision munitions. Considering the bomb loads of an aircraft like a B-2, *one aircraft* can engage *multiple targets* with a reasonable assurance of destroying them. Under the old airpower paradigm (even during the Gulf War), *multiple aircraft* had to engage a *single target* to ensure its destruction.

Advances in intelligence, surveillance, and reconnaissance (ISR) technologies are what give precision munitions actionable targets. Spaced-based systems such as reconnaissance satellites and aerial systems such as JSTARS (Joint Surveillance Target Attack Radar System) and unmanned aerial vehicles (UAVs), such as Global Hawk and the Predator, give commanders the ability to get a clearer picture of the battlefield and detect and monitor the movements of enemy forces. If special operations forces conduct intelligence, reconnaissance, and surveillance, they can send the information they gather via satellite communications systems that are virtually undetectable and that cannot be jammed.

Many of the U.S. aircraft that participated in Operation Iraqi Freedom were fighters (like the Navy and Marine Corps F/A-18s, U.S. Air Force F-16s). They flew into action from U.S. aircraft carriers, including some in the Mediterranean Sea, as well as from bases in Qatar, Kuwait, and Turkey. These attack aircraft needed aerial refueling to operate in theater and did not have extended "loiter time" over the battlefield. The targeting information provided by the improved ISR assets meant that these aircraft could be directed to targets almost immediately. Thus, each sortie usually ended in a successful attack on enemy forces.

JSTARS gave battlefield commanders the information they needed to fight the "deep battle," that is to strike Iraqi units as they moved toward U.S. ground forces. Coalition commanders created what were essentially "no-move zones" in which any vehicle on the road was considered a viable target and subjected to air attacks. If a large enough formation was detected, its area of operations was designated a "killbox" and vast amounts of firepower were brought to bear upon those units. In a few instances, in an attempt to avoid detection, Iraqi commanders ordered their men to abandon their vehicles and attack the U.S. forces on foot, a decision that led to horrific Iraqi casualties and a faster Allied advance toward Baghdad.

The precision of the coalition air effort meant that even in Baghdad and other cities, hitting crucial military and regime facilities did not require that entire neighborhoods be drenched in high explosives. Baghdad and other cities were not pulverized, huge numbers of Iraqis were not killed and injured, and there was no mass exodus of Iraqis from the cities. The huge humanitarian crisis that many critics said would result from the war never materialized.

The Iraqi strategy was, apparently, a defense-in-depth of Baghdad, the epicenter of the Ba'athist regime, shielded by remnants of the Republican Guard, the Special Republican Guard, the irregulars of the Saddam fedayeen (and the Ba'athist militias that they forced onto the battlefield), and the foreign jihadists. They threw themselves at the mechanized juggernauts of the 3rd Infantry Division and the 1st Marine Division, and were defeated in turn.

To his enormous credit, Air Force Lt. General Buzz Mosley, who was the Combined Forces Air Component Commander, took a risk and ordered U.S. aircraft to ignore worries about supposed Baghdad air defenses and offered full air support as U.S. ground forces moved into Baghdad. As U.S. ground forces made their "thunder runs" into Baghdad and later took up their positions within the city—including the international airport—they benefited from the close air support of aircraft like the A-10, an aircraft purpose-built for close air support and ground attack. These aircraft could participate so effectively in the attacks because of U.S. tactical "urban close air support" methods, in which various aircraft of differing size and equipped with differing armament are held in orbit, ready to come to the support of ground forces or hit targets of opportunity. It was a B-1 bomber flying an urban close air support mission that came within an ace of hitting Saddam Hussein as he took cover in a bunker under a Baghdad restaurant (fearful for his own security and suspicious of people around him, he left the structure after only a few minutes).

The 360-Degree Battlefield:

Updating the visual displays that showed the advance of U.S. and coalition forces into Iraq was part of our job as analysts on FOX News Channel. One bit of pioneer reporting we were able to do was to purchase commercial satellite imagery that allowed our viewers to see the battlefield as though they were flying in an airplane. That broadened the view a bit because most reporters—including the embedded reporters who did such terrific work—inevitably see the battlefield through a "straw." That image of the straw was given to us by Oliver North, who mentioned to us that that was how it struck him as an embedded reporter: reporters saw the battlefield through their own inescapably narrow view of it. Our satellite imagery could put these embedded reporter snapshots of reality into a larger context. The "Fox Flyovers," as they came to be called, emanated from the Air Force's POWERSCENE system that had been developed by Cambridge Research Associates.

Taking an even bigger view, one could see a truly revolutionary change in American military doctrine unfolding before us on the battlefield. Not long after the advance on Baghdad began, we were plotting on our maps both the Army's deep penetration, spearheaded by the 3rd Infantry Division, and the 1st Marine Division's run toward the Iraqi capital. As we did so, we realized that the advances were not on a broad, common front; instead, they were like the thrusts of two spears. Moreover, the "spear thrusts" were not operating in what some former military men would recognize as the standard mode—a two brigade- or regiment-front with a brigade or regiment held in reserve. They were moving toward their objectives as separate, apparently self-supporting units, exchanging information with each other by satellite communications. They did so with no diminution of combat power, and the results were impressive.

In the battlefield of the future, there will be no division between the forward echelon and the rear echelon. In any direction a soldier looks, there will be the "front line." This will demand new, imaginative methods for keeping units supplied—the Marines used KC-130 aircraft, landing on hastily modified highways, to do the job—and a recognition that every deployed unit is essentially a combat unit and needs to be combat-ready.

Another lesson from Operation Iraqi Freedom is that the Army and Marines no longer need to fight in the familiar "package" of the division. During the campaign, the Marines created various scratch task forces out of different units—light armored reconnaissance battalions, infantry companies—and sent them off on limited assignments. This model worked well and there is no reasonable obstacle to the creation of these types of task-oriented units on a larger scale.

Size Does Not Matter:

Since the 1980s, the U.S. military has held that it must—and will—come at any enemy with overwhelming force. Enduring conventional wisdom defines as a requirement that the U.S. forces come to the battlefield with roughly the same number of troops as the enemy, in other words, a numerical quota. The results of Operation Iraqi Freedom, however, will demand a redefinition of "overwhelming force" that looks less at numbers of troops and more at sheer firepower. In many battlefields of the future, a smaller force—well equipped, well armed, and well trained—that can move to its objectives swiftly, avoid obstacles nimbly, and deliver accurate, overwhelming firepower, will be considered an overwhelming force.

Close the Door:

As in Operation Enduring Freedom, there was a flaw in the execution of Operation Iraqi Freedom. In the fight for Tora Bora in Afghanistan, our forces effectively and impressively drove the enemy before them. There was, however, no blocking force toward which to drive, an anvil upon which the enemy could be hammered. In Operation Iraqi Freedom, the coalition left the "back door" open, specifically, the Baghdad-to-Damascus road. Over that route, jihadists were able to enter Iraq and members of Saddam Hussein's regime and, according to our sources, weapons of mass destruction and their components were able to leave the country.

"DID THE WAR IN IRAQ MAKE THE WORLD, MAKE THE UNITED STATES, SAFER?"

The answer is certainly, resoundingly, yes. Here are some benefits that we think Operation Iraqi Freedom brought to the world at large:

An End to Aggression:

The danger of Saddam Hussein's pursuit of a Greater Iraq, a threat especially to the Gulf States, is over. Also over is Iraq's thumbing its nose at UN resolutions and the Desert Storm cease-fire agreements—violations that seriously undercut the West's credibility with rogue states. These acts of "diplomatic aggression" have been punished and other states put on notice.

Iraqi WMD:

After he resigned his position, David Kay, who was in charge of the post-liberation effort to find Iraqi WMD, said that while he found no weapons per se there was ample evidence of attempts to reconstitute weapons programs and, amid reports of widespread corruption, there are abundant and well-founded suspicions that people involved in the Iraqi WMD program sold weapons and technical know-how to anybody with enough money—including terrorists. David Kay's overall assessment was that Iraq was more dangerous than we had initially envisioned. Though we are now supposed to believe that every intelligence agency in the world was wrong in its assessment that Iraq had weapons of mass destruction, we agree with Secretary Donald Rumsfeld that it is much more likely that these weapons will eventually be found; indeed, we believe that some intelligence agencies already know where they are.

Syria:

Faced with countries friendly to the United States on three fronts and with his back to the Mediterranean Sea that could bring the United States Navy and Marine Corps to his doorstep, the president of Syria, Bashar Assad, admitted to possessing weapons of mass destruction (chemical weapons), although he said he was unwilling to give them up until Israel disposes of its nuclear weapons. Although Syria has returned to its atrocious behavior, the withdrawal of its forces from Lebanon shows that it no longer considers its position unassailable. This is important because Syria punches above its weight when it comes to terrorism only because its support of terrorism goes essentially unchallenged. We are now in a position to effectively challenge it.

Libya:

Libya's longtime dictator Muammar Gaddafi took steps to reconcile with the West, including renouncing his pursuit of weapons of mass destruction, and allowing international inspectors into Libya to verify that his programs are being dismantled. His WMD program was apparently far more advanced than intelligence agencies had previously assumed. In addition, a delegation from Libya has traveled to Israel, with the purpose of talking peace—and even, perhaps, diplomatic recognition of the Jewish state. We know that Gaddafi was inspired to make these steps by watching Saddam Hussein's fall.

Israel:

With the demise of Iraq's Ba'athist regime, Israel no longer has to fear a land invasion, but must fear Iran's nuclear development. This is now Israel's most important national security concern.

Pakistan:

Despite the political risk of infuriating the strong Islamist political parties in his country, Pakistan's president Pervez Musharraf has worked hard to cooperate in the war on terror and pulled the curtain back on the corruption and secret deals of those involved with Pakistan's nuclear program, the most prominent of which was the "Father of Pakistan's Bomb," A. Q. Khan. Pakistan revealed that two senior nuclear scientists—Khan and Mohammed Farooq—used a network of middlemen operating on the black market to supply nuclear weapons technology to Iran, North Korea, and Libya for which they received millions of dollars. This further reinforces the theory of the Web of Terror and the danger these nations pose through their development of WMD and their provision of them to terrorists. Only if the governments themselves change will we be able to defeat al-Qaeda and other terrorist groups.

Since the end of the Iraq campaign, President Musharraf has met with Turkish officials to work out the terms of an agreement to counter the spread of radical Islam. He has also begun talks with India aimed at reducing tension between the countries and resolving their enduring conflict over Kashmir (where Islamist terrorists are also active and supported by many in Pakistan). Our invasion of Iraq has given Musharraf courage to go after the Islamist threat in his own country.

The United States:

Finally we need to remember what Operation Iraqi Freedom showed to the world. It showed Iraqis greeting U.S. troops, it exposed Saddam for the mass murderer that he was, and it will soon demonstrate how we have helped give birth to an Iraqi democracy that could be a model for the region. Equally important, it should remind hostile, terror-sponsoring dictators of another important lesson: don't mess with the U.S.

CHAPTER SIX

SHARPENING THE SWORD: MILITARY TRANSFORMATIONS

THE APPARENT EASE WITH WHICH the U.S. military and its allies scored impressive victories in Afghanistan and Iraq surprised many people across the world as well as in Congress, the news media, and the Muslim states—but it didn't surprise us.

The dire predictions that the U.S. military would suffer the same fate as the Soviet army in Afghanistan (bogged down in a decade-long war) and the Russian army in Chechnya (smashing cities with artillery and aerial bombardment) did not come to pass—and never would have. Now some of these misguided observers say that our victories in Iraq and Afghanistan were so swift only because our enemies were so inept. They're still wrong.

There are many reasons for why the campaigns went so well, among them: our undeniable technological edge, the superior training of our troops (including training in joint operations), and our outstanding logistical capabilities. Our coalition partners—for example, Great Britain and Australia—have provided superbly trained forces and we have received extremely important contributions—in the form of "boots on the ground," ships at sea, and diplomatic support—from other nations (e.g., Canada).

The seamlessness of our joint operations is the explanation for our successes that many outside, nonmilitary observers are most likely to miss. General Tommy Franks learned a lot about joint operations in Afghanistan with Operation Enduring Freedom and he put that knowledge to extremely good use in Operation Iraqi Freedom. His "education" was accelerated thanks to Defense Secretary Donald Rumsfeld, whose ideas about transforming our military are exactly right. Their implementation of Secretary Rumsfeld's ideas needs to be accelerated because, no matter how impressive our battlefield successes in Afghanistan and Iraq, if we are to destroy the Web of Terror, we need to do much more to improve our war-fighting capabilities.

The modern battlefield has changed dramatically. And while we are current masters of the art, we are not doing enough to reshape our military to retain our advantages. The five dimensions of modern warfare—air, land, sea, space, and information—can be, and must be, far better integrated to defeat our enemies. The goal is not only speed of execution, as demonstrated in the Afghan and Iraq campaigns, but also the disruption of the enemy's "decision cycle" so that his command-and-control apparatus completely breaks down. If that happens, an enemy army and the regime above it can be routed with a minimum of casualties. It is a form of warfare often described as "effects-based." Physical destruction of an enemy army is not the goal of combat operation; casting it into utter disarray, however, is.

HOW WE FIGHT: BLITZ WARFARE

"Blitz warfare"—not to be confused with blitzkrieg—puts a premium on quickly deployable and extremely mobile forces acting in concert. In past wars, the normal doctrine was sequential operations, conducted by individual services. So there was the "softening-up" phase conducted by Army artillery or Air Force air strikes that "prepared" a battlefield prior to the attack, then an attack phase led by ground units of the Army or Marine Corps, followed by a consolidation phase. Blitz warfare demands simultaneous operations that dramatically compress the phases of warfare. In turn, this demands *precision*, precision of

military integration and precision of targeting, which is why it is so
vital that the American military ensures it has matchless information
and precision guidance technologies. Today, we can pinpoint crucial
targets to a degree previously unimaginable, and because we can, we
can minimize civilian casualties; indeed, we can limit them to what
amount to deadly accidents. Remember that while the government sec-
tor of Baghdad was subjected to intense bombardment, most of the city
was left untouched. We were able to strike government buildings and
other enemy targets even when they were in civilian neighborhoods.

Blitz warfare is *networked* warfare. Communications technology
now allows the president of the United States to speak simultaneously
with a regional commander, the commander of an armored brigade,
and the captain of a warship—all of whom may be many hundreds of
miles from one another. It provides the battlefield commanders with
the ability to speak, exchange data, and share images with subordi-
nates and vice versa. Battle is chaos, but this networking allows information gathered by sensors on and above the battlefield to reach those
who most need it, giving them "situational awareness" of the battlefield and the areas around it. As an example, the Global Hawk
unmanned aerial vehicle has a capability called Advanced Information Architecture which enables ground forces to bring the information from the Global Hawk's sensors (infrared, television, and radar)
directly to a personal display accessory as small as an iPAQ or Palm
Pilot *within eleven seconds*. This is like giving a company commander
almost instant access to a reconnaissance satellite. While this breaks
the usual intelligence chain of dissemination, it enables our forces to
move faster, so fast that an enemy can't react effectively. That's how
we get inside the enemy's decision cycle, and so ensure that he's trying to react to our first move while we've already committed our second move. During Operation Iraqi Freedom, we had great success
integrating information from sensor systems like the aircraft-borne
Joint Surveillance and Target Attack Radar System (JSTARS);
unmanned systems like Global Hawk, Predator, and satellites; human

and signal intelligence; and the Blue Force Tracker that uses digital "ID tags" on each vehicle and satellite communications in order to help ground forces locate other friendly units. Together, these information sources gave commanders an unparalleled view of the battlefield and targeting information. And that allowed commanders to bring overwhelming firepower almost anywhere on the battlefield with speed and accuracy.

Other information warfare efforts—involving coalition intelligence, the Iraqi National Congress, and those Iraqis brave enough to aid the anti-Ba'athist cause—helped convince many Iraqi soldiers and their commanders that the right decision for them was to simply fade away from the battle.

Our development of high technology like this has made a dramatic improvement in joint warfare, but these improvements cannot stop. We need to keep pace, because it is blitz warfare that gives America a sharper sword and, thus, greater diplomatic clout, which means saving lives and improving our national security. It is blitz warfare that can liberate North Korea with much less damage and loss of life than many analysts think—and that, even short of war, can bring North Korea to the bargaining table ready to surrender its WMD capability.

THE WEAPONS WE NEED

The battlefield of the future will not conform to the U.S. order of battle just because the Pentagon wishes it were so. We cannot think in terms of tinkering with the military structure leftover from the Cold War, adding a little here, taking away a little there. We need a thorough transformation—which is, in fact, one of the stated goals of the Bush administration.

Donald Rumsfeld's business experience, his reputation as a cost-cutter and efficiency specialist, and, most of all, his readiness to embrace high technology, Special Forces units, integrated "actionable" intelligence, joint operations, and innovative military thinking

make him the right man for the job. What our military needs is not
greater numbers but an effort to "balance the force" so that there is a
much higher proportion of war fighters in active, Guard, and Reserve
units; so that more of our units are mobile and capable of quick
response; and so that we make the utmost use of high technology,
because such technology is crucial to making our lean and often out-
numbered forces much more lethal than their adversaries.

I   I   I   I   I   I   I   I   I

The first item on the Transformation "To Do" list is to reshape the
military in terms of expeditionary forces. During the Cold War, the
Navy and the Marine Corps deployed forces on a regular basis to the
Pacific, the Mediterranean, and other areas around the world, often
in aircraft carrier task forces, later in aircraft carrier battle groups and
Marine Amphibious Units, and later, in Marine Expeditionary Units.
Today, the Navy and the Marines remain organized for rapid
embarkation and deployment. Even though the Marines have heavy
equipment and weapons, their largest and "heaviest" units are
"medium" at best.

Even more important than the "portability" of Marine Corps and
Navy units is their "expeditionary" organizational structure and
mindset. The Navy sends aircraft carrier battle groups (CVBGs) around
the world and Marines often embark as part of a Marine Expeditionary
Unit (MEU)—a reinforced infantry battalion that has its own organic
artillery, aviation (a combined helicopter squadron and six Harrier
Vertical and/or Short Take-off and Landing, VSTOL, jets), and supply
and maintenance units—on board a three-ship Navy amphibious
ready group (ARG). The sailors and Marines attached to a CVBG or an
ARG-MEU team know they will face a regular schedule of training,
"work-ups," deployment, and return. They also have a rough idea of
when they will deploy, know where they will be deployed (at least
initially), and are mindful that they might be required to perform any

number of tasks during their deployment. Marines and sailors accept all that as part of what they do.

Earlier this decade, the Navy and the Marine Corps developed a new formation that provides improved capabilities for the MEU-ARG team: the expeditionary strike group (ESG). The basic three-ship ARG and its embarked Marines are "married" to a guided missile cruiser, two other surface combatants (cruisers, destroyers, or frigates), an attack submarine, and a P-3 Orion maritime patrol aircraft. These assets provide greater offensive strength in the form of the ships' cruise missiles and guns and better defensive capabilities as well. The current Chief of Naval Operations, Admiral Vern Clark, has introduced the concept of "surge operations" with his CVBGs, which allows the Navy to rapidly bring six carriers to a theater of operations (as was done in Operation Iraqi Freedom).

The U.S. Air Force has embraced the expeditionary concept as well, albeit in a different mode from that of the Navy and the Marine Corps. The demands placed on the Air Force by Operation Northern Watch and Operation Southern Watch—the enforcement of no-fly zones over northern and southern Iraq—overstretched the service and prompted justifiable complaints from pilots and other personnel about the strains on personnel and machines. So the Air Force reformulated the entire service as an "expeditionary air and space force" capable of fielding ten "air and space expeditionary forces." Essentially, these ten "AEFs" are all of roughly equal combat power and draw personnel and equipment from all over the Air Force for possible deployment. Moreover, almost every uniformed member of the Air Force—officer and enlisted alike—knows he or she is liable for service with an AEF on a deployment of up to fifteen months. As with the Navy and Marine Corps, this certain knowledge of expected duty makes for better morale.

The Air Force is used to operating out of bases with extensive infrastructure. In the new warfare, such bases won't always be available. The campaign in Afghanistan brought home to the Air Force the need to establish and operate new bases in forward areas, and to be able to do so at short notice. The Air Force got the message. Between February 2003 and April 2003, the Air Force established a dozen bases in the Persian Gulf region, including five established in Iraq during Operation Iraqi Freedom.

Until Afghanistan and Iraq, the heavy units of the Army had not had much recent expeditionary warfare experience, stationed as they long had been in Europe during the Cold War and in South Korea, where their mission was (or is) to stop massive ground offensives. The Army has had, however, ample experience in peacekeeping operations, sending units to Bosnia, the Sinai Peninsula, and elsewhere.

Still, it is telling that the Army's initial reaction to Special Forces successes in Afghanistan was to follow up by deploying a heavy, mechanized force. The Army still thinks in terms of the Cold War conventional operations it has long trained for, relying on a long logistical tail and a large base structure in the United States and Europe. But that won't do for the War on Terror. Thankfully, the Army's chief of staff, General Peter Schoomaker, whose background is in special operations and light infantry, is continuing to rework the Army's approach to expeditionary warfare and make its units more able to participate in joint expeditionary operations. We strongly endorse General Schoomaker's transformation of the Army and are hopeful that whenever he retires his successor keeps the Army moving in the right direction.

The military needs to continue to think in terms of expeditionary warfare; it also needs to keep thinking about how to wring more combat power out of our force structure. Many in Congress want to expand the armed forces, particularly the Army and the Marine Corps. We agree that there is some room to expand these services to relieve the commitments of active-duty, Guard, and Reserve units in Iraq, Afghanistan, and elsewhere. However, we firmly believe that the sense of being overburdened does not stem from a lack of personnel, but because our armed forces have too many tasks that go beyond the waging of war. Secretary Rumsfeld already has identified approximately 245,000 jobs across the Department of Defense that could be outsourced to contractors. Our recommendation: outsource the jobs, use the savings to improve the lot of the "trigger pullers," and create new frontline fighting units while phasing out paper-pushing ones. In other words, change the "tail to tooth" ratio so there is less tail and more tooth.

Personnel are the highest priced item in the Department of Defense budget, so rather than reflexively expand the number of billets, the Pentagon should make better and more efficient use of the current personnel levels. The Army should follow the lead of the Air Force, which within its Air and Space Expeditionary Forces makes every member of, say, the Air Staff in the Pentagon liable for deployment. The advantage of this is that it trims the support tail of the force and eliminates occupational redundancy. For example, doctors, nurses, and medics who are stationed at the Walter Reed Army Hospital or the Brooks Army Medical Center should be part of an "expeditionary medical unit" that could be deployed as an "expeditionary support element." *Every* member of the armed forces should be combat zone deployable. If they aren't, their function should be outsourced, or eliminated.

Another way to get greater combat power out of the current force structure is to change the way the Army and Marine Corps are structured for combat. First, the Army needs to get "lighter"—that is to say, have smaller and less layered headquarters and fewer armored, mechanized infantry, field artillery, and air defense artillery units in its inventory. That means that the Army might not need as many tanks as it currently has in its inventory or as many self-propelled artillery pieces. Heavy forces are still needed and vitally important, but lighter units in expeditionary forces should be the priority, because they are more likely to see combat against the threats we face now. And as part of that restructuring the Army will need to enlarge its Special Forces and focus to a greater degree on unconventional warfare and integrating with the CIA. The Army must get away from the notion of fighting in division-sized elements (and larger) and think more in terms of fighting brigades or combat groups that have a mix of light, medium, and heavy forces. Taking a cue from the Marine Corps, the Army must ensure that any Army unit operating in the joint expeditionary warfare environment will be capable of independent operations and possessed of adequate air and ground mobility, firepower, and combat service support.

This isn't a new idea. In World War II, the U.S. Army's armored divisions in northwestern Europe adopted an organization that divided their striking forces into two combined-arms teams of roughly equivalent structures known as "combat commands." In World War II and Korea, the Army also developed units known as "regimental combat teams." In both instances, these formations were configured for independent combat operations. Even today the Army has Separate Infantry Brigades (like the 173rd Airborne Brigade which secured the northern front area of Iraq) that are very capable units.

What the Army needs are deployable "brigade combat groups," of five thousand troops—including light infantry, airborne or air assault forces, and/or armor/mechanized units/artillery with a support brigade integrated into joint expeditionary forces. For soldiers, the notion of fixed deployments must be as familiar as it is for sailors and Marines. A set deployment schedule not only improves joint operations combat training but also is more conducive to family stability, morale, and personnel retention than are the seemingly endless deployments of a few unfortunate units. Also as an aid to morale and performance, units—not individual soldiers rotating in and out— should be sent on deployments.

The Army needs to keep moving to reduce Cold War headquarters and structures, increase brigade-based maneuver elements, and thoroughly restructure Guard and Reserve components. We strongly endorse the Army's initiative in this area.

In order to restructure our Guard and Reserve components properly, we need to change public attitudes about these forces, attitudes left over from the Cold War. The Guard and Reserves are not comical "weekend warriors." These men and women have served all over the world, making invaluable contributions to the war effort. Some have paid the ultimate price. We know Reserve officers, non-commissioned officers, and enlisted men who have performed such duties as ensuring a smooth flow of ammunition from an Army arsenal, training Iraqi soldiers, engaging in close combat in the most grueling conditions in Iraq, and leading a civil affairs effort in the countryside of Afghanistan. Indeed, if it were not for the service of these citizen-soldiers—so often characterized by experience and maturity—our forces would have been severely hamstrung in the campaigns we have conducted since September 2001.

If the regular forces are reconfigured as expeditionary forces, it makes sense for many "heavy" armor and artillery units to become the province of the National Guard and Reserve. Moreover, given the nature of the war on terror, other units well represented in the reserves— military police and intelligence units—would be better placed in the regular forces.

Another issue confronting the U.S. military is what to do with its Cold War basing structure. Even after widespread base closings in the 1990s, many military facilities in the United States are of dubious value. In general, as far as domestic basing is concerned, the chief question policymakers need to ask is whether the deployable units at the base are within quick reach of proper transport facilities. If not, the base should be closed and the units moved to another base.

Overseas—and in Europe especially—if you looked at a map of American bases you might think that the Cold War was still on. In the Pacific theater, because of the North Korean threat, we still need our deployments in Japan and we are already restructuring our system of bases in South Korea. Many European bases—with a few significant exceptions, like Ramstein Air Base in Germany—can be closed, since Europe is no longer a likely battlefield for the United States.

Much more important is to have a chain of forward operating bases ("lily pads") in Central Asia, South Asia, and the Middle East.

Because the units stationed on them would be rotating through on a fixed deployment cycle or using them for sustained combat operations, there would be no need to develop dependent housing and other infrastructure that makes many of the old Cold War bases so expensive.

The U.S. military also faces a problem with "capitalization." There are some fantastic items of high-tech equipment now available to our men and women in the field. The trouble is that all too often, there is not enough of it to go around. All of the services are facing block obsolescence of at least some equipment. Some vehicles and aircraft are decades old and their replacements are very slowly arriving in the field. Even when new equipment is available, it often does not replace older equipment on a one-for-one basis. The lack of sufficient numbers of airborne tankers borders on criminal neglect. We cannot hope to extend U.S. and allied airpower wherever and whenever we need it without a much more robust aerial refueling capability. To recapitalize its current force structure, the Department of Defense needs to spend about $125 billion annually. Combat and support operations in the war on terror are consuming most, if not all, of the increases in the defense budget. Because our forces now operate at a much higher operational tempo—with dramatic increases in combat operations—and because during the 1990s modernization spending averaged around $50 billion per year, the shortfall in modernization expenditures probably hovers around $500 billion.

One way to overcome this hurdle is with smaller units using new and more effective technologies. For example, using the unmanned Global Hawk in place of Navy P-3s for broad-area maritime surveillance and in place of U-2s for surveillance and reconnaissance would enable Defense to save at least one billion dollars per year.

Of course, $1 billion might not seem much in a huge defense budget that runs into the hundreds of billions, but consider how much ammunition the Army could buy for $1 billion, how much more fuel the Air Force could buy for $1 billion, and you can see why it's important for the Pentagon to ensure that it makes the best possible use of every dollar. Getting the most bang for the buck isn't just a cliché, it's the way military planners and congressional budget-setters have to think. And if done properly, as we've outlined here, it can actually sharpen our nation's sword to an even keener edge.

CHAPTER SEVEN

BURNISHING THE SHIELD

IN THE GOLDEN AGE OF THE GREEK city-states, when the likes of Athens and Sparta were at the zenith of their power and glory, the dominant force on the battlefields of ancient Greece was the heavy infantryman, the hoplite. The hoplite's weapons were valuable to him because they were what he used to strike at his enemies; likewise his helmet because it protected his head and face from missiles and blows. The bronze shield, however, had an almost mystical importance to these citizen-soldiers. It was an important personal possession; it often was inherited, and a hoplite's mother or wife placed good-luck totems inside the shield's bowl. Legend has it that Spartan wives and mothers sternly reminded their sons and husbands of their duty to Sparta by telling the men to come home with their shields or on them. A hoplite considered the loss of his shield to be a great disgrace.

On the battlefield, the shield did not protect its owner per se but the man to his left; therefore, every soldier in formation depended on the man next to him. This relationship of trust and mutual defense in an infantry formation became a metaphor for the hoplites and their relationship with the city-states. If the hoplites failed, they were guilty of letting their larger shield slip, and thus endangering the city-state.

To the enemy, advancing hoplites appeared as a wall of shields. Above those shields was a forest of spears that, at a given signal, came

down, pointing toward the enemy. In order to instill discipline and
pride in their men as well as to lend their advancing formation an
even more fearsome aspect, commanders often would order their men
to burnish their shields to a bright shine before battle.

We've spoken of the need to transform the U.S. military. If you will,
that was sharpening the sword. Now, we want to discuss how to burnish the shield.

A NEW ALLIANCE

In times of war, any nation automatically looks for allies. In World
War I, the British and the French desperately hoped that the Americans
would arrive in time to turn the tide against the Kaiser and actively
worked to accelerate U.S. entrance into that conflict. In June 1941,
Winston Churchill swallowed his decades-long hatred of Soviet Communism and gladly welcomed the Soviet Union into the war against
the Nazis. In the late 1940s, the United States led the effort to create
alliances that would act as bulwarks against the Soviet Union and successfully created not only NATO, but also the Central Treaty Organization (CENTO) and the Southeast Asia Treaty Organization (SEATO).

In the War on Terror, the United States never has gone it alone—and
never will. Soon after the attacks of September 11, 2001, NATO
affirmed its founding principle that an attack on one is an attack on
all, and NATO played (and still plays) an important role in Afghanistan. Although some of the countries that had participated in the
Afghan campaign refused to participate in the liberation of Iraq, the
United States still has been able to count on the assistance of such
countries as Britain, Australia, Japan, South Korea, the Philippines,
Thailand, Italy, Spain, Poland, Denmark, Hungary, Bulgaria, Ukraine,
Romania, the Netherlands, Norway, El Salvador, and nearly twenty
other countries.

This alliance, at times called the "coalition of the willing," doesn't
exist as an institution, although many of its members are formally

linked to us by treaty, but is an active reality. Another example of such
an informal institution is the U.S.-led Proliferation Security Initiative
(PSI). When Libya agreed to give up its nuclear weapons program after
Operation Iraqi Freedom, it did so *not* because of the diplomatic
efforts of the UN or NATO, but because of British and American diplomatic efforts coordinated through the instrument of the PSI. The PSI
is committed to preventing the proliferation of WMD and to do so by
the interdiction of WMD weapons, delivery systems, components, and
materials. The PSI has no formal organization; as one administration
official told the *Wall Street Journal*, it is "an activity, not an organization." This loose group of nations dedicated to counter-proliferation
is centered on sixteen countries—Australia, Canada, Denmark, the
Netherlands, the United Kingdom, Poland, France, Portugal, Germany,
Spain, Italy, Singapore, Turkey, Japan, Norway, and the United
States—but as many as fifty nations have stated that they agree with
the PSI's principles and will lend aid whenever they are needed.

The fact that the PSI is an "activity," not an organization, means
that it is dedicated to action, not bureaucracy. And the cliché is true:
Actions speak louder than words. In September 2003, a freighter,
bound for Libya and carrying parts used in the machinery used to
enrich uranium, was diverted to an Italian port. There, police and
customs officials searched the ship and seized its cargo. In August
2003, at the request of the United States, port officials in Taiwan
boarded a freighter headed to North Korea and confiscated its cargo—
ingredients for chemical weapons. These cooperative actions between
states committed to preventing weapons proliferation are all that is
needed to get the job done. What the war on terror does not need is a
formal alliance or organization that risks creating *another* bureaucracy to support it.

At most, what would be useful is a *short* document—no more than
one page—called "The Freedom from Terrorism Charter," laying out
our commitment to destroy the regimes that make up the Web of Terror and foster the creation of free and open societies in their place.

Countries that are demonstrably committed to democratic values and to defeating the Web of Terror can sign it as a statement of common principles. As an informal alliance, it would be flexible to varying strategic needs, and provide a global answer to the question of why we fight.

Along with the sixteen participants in the PSI, we should solicit a signature from India—first, because it is the world's largest democracy; second, because it is geo-strategically pivotal; third, because it is economically and technologically advanced; fourth, because it has a large and capable military (with substantial combat experience) and a first-rate intelligence service. And it is a natural ally against radical Islam.

For those who are keen on creating another formal alliance, we would ask them: "What treaty bound the Grand Alliance of World War II—the United States, the United Kingdom, and the Soviet Union—from December 1941 to September 1945?" Common interests are what make an alliance real, not vast bureaucracies churning out masses of paperwork.

REFORMING AMERICAN DIPLOMACY

Now, almost five years after the war began, the State Department needs a transformation as sweeping as the one now under way in the Pentagon. Its structure is at least fifteen years out of date because it still places foreign service officers—the State Department's frontline diplomats—in Western Europe rather than in countries of increasing power, influence, and importance such as China and India. For example, when Secretary of State Condoleezza Rice announced her reform plan in January 2005, she pointed out that the number of State Department personnel in Germany, a country of eighty-two million people, is roughly equal to the number of personnel in India, a country with a population of one billion.

Just as important is the reason for reform of the State Department culture. Currently, the American diplomatic culture values "process" (like a "peace process") no matter how negligible the results. It values "engagement" with hostile countries even if engagement gets us nothing. It values diplomatic courtesy to hostile countries even if such courtesy disheartens and undercuts democratic opposition groups that are our natural friends and allies.

Secretary Rice issued a long overdue reminder to American diplomats—and those in the news media, academia, think tanks, and Congress who admire the old Foggy Bottom culture—that the United States is at war and that the State Department should think of itself as an institution on the front line of the war's *political* front. She pointedly reminded them that American diplomats are not sent abroad to merely observe and report—although that is part and parcel of diplomacy—but to aggressively advance American policy. And the president and secretary of state should make it a priority to appoint and to fire administration officials according to their ability to absorb and enact that message.

America's diplomats cannot be afraid to speak frank truths to the countries to which they are assigned, to ensure that American aid serves American interests (and not line foreign bureaucrats' pockets), and to make America's case for freedom to the country at large, using the local media. We cannot have diplomats hiding in bunkers or practicing quiet diplomacy alone. In this war, they must be public figures, taking risks like our service men and women, because like them, they are on the front line of a war.

Secretary Rice calls it "transformational diplomacy": the reapportionment of our diplomatic resources and the insistence that U.S. diplomats become more active in explaining the American perspective and promoting American policies wherever they represent our country. We certainly hope that foreign service officers follow Secretary Rice's leadership, embrace her ideas about reshaping American diplomacy, and begin to rework their own internal culture. This way, the State Department will become a more vigorous and effective player in the war. Ensuring this will almost certainly take close supervision and forceful leadership; historically, foreign service officers often have displayed a marked reluctance to follow the lead of presidents.

Like the Cold War, the war on terror is very much a war of ideas; therefore, it is imperative that the U.S. government strengthen its public diplomacy effort. In November 2002, Norman Pattiz, chairman of Westwood One and a member of the U.S. Broadcasting Board of Governors, said, "In terms of the Middle East, there is a media war going on. The weapons of that war are hate radio, disinformation, incitement to violence, government censorship, and journalistic self-censorship." To its credit, the United States has not shied away from this particular battlefield, establishing one station aimed at Iran, Radio Azadi ("Freedom"), in 1998, and one aimed at the broader region, Radio Sawa ("Together"), in July 2002, under the auspices of the U.S. Broadcasting Board of Governors, which is responsible for such services as Radio Liberty, Radio Free Asia, and the Voice of America.

The story of Radio Azadi—renamed Radio Farda ("Tomorrow") in December 2002—is instructive. The service began broadcasting to Iran in 1998, albeit a mere thirty minutes a day. Predictably, the mullahs of Iran decried it as a "CIA plot" and banned Iranians from making any contact with the service. The people of Iran do not lack for broadcast choices; therefore, many in and out of Iran were skeptical about Radio Azadi's ability to attract and retain an audience. Radio Azadi had prepared well, however—recruiting journalists with experience in Iran, installing an Iranian editor and an energetic staff of young producers and broadcasters in studios in Prague, and adhering to a neutral tone in its newscasts. It soon carved out a niche in the Iran "market" and expanded its program offerings and its broadcast day. Over time, more Iranian academics, artists, students, and intellectuals— inside and outside Iran—began appearing on the show, and consequently Radio Azadi's credibility and audience grew steadily.

Radio Sawa has had its growing pains. Aimed at young people (age fifteen to thirty), its popular music programming gained it a wide audience. However, some in and out of the region have criticized it for insufficient substance and for having insufficient gravity. Whether or not that criticism is fair, Radio Sawa is well worth the effort, since the alternative—allowing state-controlled media and the likes of al-Jazeera a free hand to spin lies about the United States and its policies—is unacceptable.

FIVE FREEDOMS

We cannot defeat the Web of Terror solely by military means. We must broadcast to the people of these countries a message of liberation and hope, of freedom and opportunity, of a better life that lies not in terrorism and war but in free markets and democratic governments that respect all peoples and all faiths. Diplomacy with the regimes in question has both its uses and its limits.

But we need to speak directly to the people as well. The infamous al-Jazeera, dozens of state-run radio and television channels, and hundreds of newspapers and magazines in the Islamic world spread anti-Western news and, intentionally or unintentionally, inculcate hatred toward it. We need an effective countervoice. Our popular culture, which strikes many Muslims as poisonous, cannot do the job on its own, and can even be counterproductive. We need a massive infusion of American media, geared to an Islamic audience, that states the case for peace and freedom.

An illustration of how much work we have to do in this matter came to our attention in January 2006. The FOX News Channel's Brit Hume reported that during the annual *haj*, when millions of Muslims go to Mecca as pilgrims, the top cleric in Saudi Arabia, Sheik Abdulaziz al-Sheik, publicly declared, "O, Muslim nation, there is a war against our creed, against our culture under the pretext of fighting terrorism. We should stand firm and united in protecting our religion."

During the same event, the sheik declared, "Islam's enemies want to empty our religion from its contents and its meaning. But the soldiers of God will be victorious."

Only a few weeks later, we met Dr. Tawfik Hamid, an Egyptian who had adhered to radical Islam as a young man and who had prayed in the same mosque as al-Qaeda's second-in-command, Ayman al-Zawahiri. Hamid asserted that there is a deep well of sympathy and support for Islamist terrorism among Muslims, stemming from the dominance of fundamentalist and triumphalist views in mosques and other Islamic institutions. These views, according to him, are based on a skewed interpretation of sacred Islamic texts.

Both incidents reveal the need for a much more serious approach to our public diplomacy, one that does not shy away from taking radicalism head-on. Our diplomacy must send a much more serious message, one that appeals morally to Muslim men and women, one that shows them the virtues—not just the well-known vices—of Western culture.

For this effort to succeed, the message must speak to the fundamental yearning of every human being for a life that is free from fear and want. We must make the case that democratic governance, an open economy, and a tolerant culture are the best means to fulfill this yearning and to achieve long-lasting peace and prosperity.

Many Islamist websites issue dire warnings about the effects of secular democracy on the moral and social fabric of any Muslim nation so foolish as to adopt it. To answer this argument, we have, thankfully, the example of Turkey; and if we succeed in Iraq, we will have the example of Iraq. But fundamentally we need to show that freedom is not a synonym for libertinism and license.

Immediately before World War II, Franklin Roosevelt summed up what the United States was defending in terms of freedoms: Freedom of Speech, Freedom from Fear, Freedom from Want, and Freedom of Religion, which inspired Norman Rockwell's famous paintings illustrating the freedoms. We suggest that today America needs to internationally broadcast its support for the Five Freedoms.

Freedom of Education:

In far too many places in the Middle East, the primary mission of the schools is political indoctrination. In Iraq before its liberation, the cult of Saddam Hussein was introduced in primary schools, reinforced through the universities, and then continued for a lifetime through the efforts of the state-run media. In their schools, Palestinian children are taught to hate Israelis—and Jews in general—from their earliest years. In many of the *madrassas* of Pakistan, where young men are sent to learn the Koran, students receive a radical Islamist political message (most of the Pakistanis who fought for the Taliban were recruited directly from these schools). We should make clear to Muslim parents that freedom of education means giving their children employable skills and hope for a better future, as well as giving parents the opportunity to pass *their* values, rather than those of an oppressive regime or a group of inflexible fundamentalists, on to their children.

Freedom of the Economy:

One of the reasons so many states in the Muslim world have failed so miserably is that they have little or no economic freedom. Capitalism is an imperfect system, but it indisputably creates economic prosperity. To flourish, however, it requires freedom and the rule of law.

In many Muslim countries, large industries are controlled by the state, their assets and incomes funneled to members of the ruling party or family and their cronies. In Saudi Arabia, Robert Baer reports in his book *Sleeping with the Devil*, businessmen are constantly worried not about their companies' potential failure but about their potential success. Apparently, some members of the royal family have a habit of forcing successful businessmen to sell their companies to them, usually well below market value. The Palestinian Authority's economic system is one in which people become wealthy because they have close connections with the organization's leadership or have access to the hundreds of millions of dollars in direct foreign aid provided to the Palestinian Authority by many countries. Unfortunately for Palestinians, the only truly successful Palestinian executives are those who live and work in such places as Canada and the United States.

We need to broadcast to the Muslim world that we support private property. That's a message that will resonate. Defining freedom as freedom to own your own land and business independent of state depredations will be popular—and it is necessary for economic and political reform and progress.

Freedom of Information:

When we traveled to Iraq in 2003, one of the most heartening things we encountered was the plethora of publications that had sprung up in the country. As Iraq's experience shows—and as we know from the Cold War—people living in closed societies yearn for freedom of information. We need to do what we can to encourage alternative information outlets.

We should demonstrate this freedom by using more traditional media outlets—magazines, newspapers, television, and radio—and the "new media" outlets—satellite television and radio, voice-over Internet, blogs, and DVDs—to get our messages out to the Muslim world. It is instructive to remember that one of the most effective means that the opposition to the Shah of Iran used to spread its message was the seemingly humble audiocassette.

Freedom of the Person:

In the United States and other Western countries, the freedom to live where we like, to pursue any career, and to participate in a whole range of activities—civic, religious, and charitable—without worry about state approval or interference is taken as a given. But in much of the Muslim world, people are treated as chattels of the ruling party or cabal or are intimidated by terrorists and thugs. It is almost certain, therefore, that an expansive but limited ideal of personal freedom (including a freedom of religious conscience) will be widely welcomed.

Freedom of Governance:

Much of the Muslim world brims with frustration and resentment toward rigid, authoritarian governments. We need to show that democratic government will give the people the authority to enact change peacefully through the legislative process and to hold their own elected officials accountable. Getting the Muslim world to focus on democratic domestic politics is the great antidote to what happens now: the projection of radicalized Muslim hatred outward in the form of terrorism. We need to encourage democratization throughout the Muslim world, and to ensure that people have confidence in their electoral system, the United States—or, if necessary, the UN—should be willing to monitor and verify elections, until the efficacy and resilience of democracy has been proved to the people.

There is every chance that freedom and democracy will put down roots in countries like Iraq and even Saudi Arabia. Writing in the *Weekly Standard* in the summer of 2003, the Iranian journalist and author Amir Taheri challenged the idea that there is no Islamic tradition of citizenship. He pointed out that since the tenth and eleventh centuries, there has been a body of Islamic thought that allows for nonauthoritarian governments. At least one Muslim scholar who lived and wrote in the fourteenth century discussed "a secular bond between citizens." One scholar might not impress—except when you stop to consider that many of the Islamist terror groups derive their raison d'être from the writings of a single *thirteenth-century* scholar.

There have been more recent examples of the establishment of democratic institutions—in Morocco, for instance. Even Iran's situation speaks to the potential for a democratic revolution in the region. Were it not for the mullahs' determination to hold on to power and maintain their rigid control over state institutions, including the military and security forces, Iran probably would have a second, more peaceful revolution at the ballot box.

Right now, two Gulf States, Bahrain and Qatar, are democratizing. Since 2001, the ruling family of Bahrain—the al-Khalifas—has been transforming the country from an emirate into a constitutional monarchy. Admittedly, the family still maintains considerable power—the king's uncle is prime minister—but Bahrain has taken the first steps to establish a working democratic state. In Qatar, the monarch, Sheikh Hamad bin Khalifa al-Thani, has embarked on a broad program of liberalization and gradual reform. A loosening of press restrictions led to the establishment of al-Jazeera, a mixed blessing to be sure, but al-Jazeera is not state-controlled and shows other Gulf States that press freedom need not endanger their governments. The emir's wife plays a prominent and public role in the country, lending her patronage to environmental and educational projects. Women in Qatar are allowed to vote and hold public office.

Morocco remains an exceptionally encouraging success story. Since ascending the throne in 1999, King Mohammed VI—who describes himself as a "citizen king," his people's "first servant"—has moved the government toward a constitutional monarchy, its economy toward a more open system, and its law and society toward one in which Islam is a liberating force that guarantees civil liberties and women's rights. The reforms have been embraced by all facets of Moroccan society, including the putative Islamist political parties. In September 2002, Morocco held its first general election and twenty-six political parties took part. Even after the Islamist suicide bombings in Casablanca in 2003, Morocco went ahead with local elections. Morocco, however, is not sanguine about the threat of Wahhabism. Its security forces have arrested many members of the radical Moroccan Islamic Combatant Group since the 2003 bombings and, in November 2005, rolled up a seventeen-member terrorist cell with connections to al-Qaeda. Quoted in a January 2006 edition of the German news magazine *Der Spiegel*, a female Moroccan religious scholar said approvingly, "We want to prevent our young people from being led astray." While the examples of Morocco, Qatar, and Bahrain might not satisfy some advocates of democracy, they just might provide examples to the House of Saud that political reforms do not necessarily mean the end of a dynasty.

The notion that a people cannot "handle" democratic ideas if they have been yoked to tyranny has diminishing credibility in our information age. Many people in the Middle East have been exposed to information about democratic government, through either direct experience or the ever more popular means of satellite TV and the Internet. The education level in these countries often is relatively high, and often there is a substantial middle class who could make the transition from authoritarian government to democratic government a relatively smooth one. As to the reaction of ordinary people to democracy, there are many examples of individuals emerging from under authoritarian rule and enthusiastically embracing democracy. Indeed, one of the more striking images of the 1990s was of the long lines at the polls in South Africa when that country first held truly free and open elections. People who had never voted before, whose direct experience with government probably had been with security police enforcing apartheid, stood for hours in order to cast their votes.

Those who warn us that "culture" will prevent people in the Middle East from embracing the Five Freedoms disregard the example of immigrants from the Middle East, North Africa, and southern Asia to Western Europe, the United States, and Canada—immigrants who have taken quickly to Western freedoms and democratic institutions, and prospered in market economies. We will have succeeded in defeating the Web of Terror when the freedom and success that Muslim immigrants find in the West can be replicated in the countries from which they came.

Another option to encourage that development is the reestablishment of the U.S. Information Agency, which served as America's public relations agency during the Cold War. From 1953 to the late 1990s, when the State Department absorbed it, the USIA managed educational, cultural, and information programs about the United States. A "new" USIA would present to the world those facets of American life that our invasive popular culture does not always show in the best of lights (if it shows them at all). It would explain American perspectives on current events and historical ones, describe how government and politics work in the United States, and show how the Five Freedoms apply in the United States. Based on the security situation in the particular countries, the USIA could reestablish the American cultural centers and libraries that were ubiquitous during the Cold War or extend the "American room" program begun in the 1990s that establishes an area in public libraries dedicated to American literature, history, and culture.

We are mindful of the difficulties involved in breaking through the "static" of state-owned media in the Middle East and countering the effects of decades of propaganda. Based on the many outlandish conspiracy theories we have encountered in the Middle East's official media, our opinion is that it will not be easy getting the new USIA and the new broadcast service accepted as authoritative sources of news and information. Of course, the other side of that statement is that, because of the dubious veracity of state-run and state-controlled news media outlets in the Middle East, millions upon millions of people are hungry for news they can trust.

ON THE HOME FRONT

A necessary reform is the creation of a branch of the federal judiciary known as Special Terrorist Courts, to expedite trials related to terrorism and keep them secure. In these courts, suspects initially classed as "enemy combatants" or criminals abetting terrorism would face a panel of three judges. The judges would both preside over the trials (with prosecuting and defense attorneys) and render the verdicts. There would be no juries (juries pose too many security-related risks) and there would be special rules to protect secret intelligence and counterintelligence information presented as evidence, protect witnesses who might be intelligence or law-enforcement agents or former terrorists, and provide security for judges and prosecutors. Another panel of judges would choose defense attorneys from volunteers who have substantial experience in criminal prosecution at the federal level; these attorneys would be vetted thoroughly and subjected to periodic security checks.

Congress also needs to get serious about laying out in detail the special powers that federal authorities can legally exercise, and that can be extended by Congress as necessary, in order to protect lives and maintain public order in case of a terrorist emergency. Beyond that, as part of the act, Congress and the president should develop and codify in *law* the process by which the United States government would reconstitute itself quickly after a nuclear or other devastating attack on Washington by terrorists.

Laws passed in the mid-1960s concerning the succession to the presidency make that aspect of our government's survival relatively clear. The Twenty-fifth Amendment lays out the process by which the president of the United States can name a vice president if that office becomes vacant and the vice president can serve as acting president if the president is incapacitated. The Constitution allows governors to fill vacant Senate seats by appointment. There is, however, no legal or constitutional mechanism to fill vacancies in the House of Representatives by appointment in case of a national emergency. To ensure that the U.S. government can be rebuilt promptly after a strike on the nation's capital, the Constitution needs to be amended to allow state governors to fill vacant seats of the U.S. House of Representatives by appointment, with such appointments limited to members of the same party as the member who has died or been incapacitated. Similarly, Congress should enact a law that specifies a sequence of judicial seniority among federal courts so that automatic appointment can fill the benches of the Supreme Court in case of a terrorist strike. And finally, Congress should look to dispersing the various constituent federal departments and agencies that deal with national security.

We shouldn't make ourselves an inviting target. The war on terror will be conducted not just with the sword. We need the strong shield that comes with a prudent defense and fallback strategies that plan for the worst. This preparation, and having workable strategies to deal with worst-case scenarios, is one of the best ways of preventing them from happening.

PART THREE

WHY WE FIGHT

CHAPTER EIGHT

THE GREAT CAUSE

W E ALWAYS FOUND—and still find—tiresome the charge that the United States and its allies conducted the campaign in Iraq "for oil." If Iraq's oil was all we wanted, there was a very simple way to get it: lift the embargo on Iraqi oil exports. This is so obvious that we can only imagine that protesters who scream "no blood for oil" are either astonishingly stupid or cynically disingenuous.

We had expected that, during the 2004 presidential election campaign, the Democrats would make the Bush administration's conduct of the war on terror a major issue, and that our successes would be rhetorically converted into defeats. After the election was over, we expected that these fevered charges would fade, replaced by an acknowledgment of the fact that the war in Iraq had rid the world of a murderous tyranny that sponsored terrorists, threatened its neighbors, and killed tens of thousands of the people it ruled.

As we write this update, however, the rhetoric against the campaign in Iraq has remained as heated as it was during the election, and allegedly responsible politicians from both parties have urged a cut-and-run policy regarding the war.

Critics of the Iraq campaign are fond of comparing it to the Vietnam War. They confidently—and usually mistakenly—draw parallels between the events and personalities of Vietnam and those of Iraq, and just as confidently predict ultimate failure. All too often, their historical memory fails them, however, regarding the effects that our defeats in Vietnam and Cambodia had on American security, prestige, and influence.

Our defeat in South Vietnam conveyed the message that although America could be not stopped by force of arms, it could be beaten by political pressure and a weakening of public will. It was a clear statement that the rhetoric about our willingness to "bear any burden" in the Cold War was empty. It also put our allies all over the world on notice that we would abandon them if we thought the conditions right—and that we could convince ourselves cutting and running really was "peace with honor." Simply put, the surrender of 1975 was the nadir of American power in the twentieth century.

The effects of abandoning Iraq would be far worse.

Abandoning Iraq would hand radical Islamists a victory of far greater value than the events of September 11, 2001, might have given them. With immense credibility, they could boast that they had defeated the United States. Our abandonment of Iraq would lend enormous credence to the radical Islamists' assertion that Americans are weaklings with no stomach for a prolonged fight, that we were unable to face a determined onslaught of righteous "holy warriors," and that we pressured our bickering, weak-willed political leaders to cut and run. Our surrender—and that is what it would be—would be taken as prima facie evidence that the future belonged to those who wanted to impose the stern, pitiless, and inflexible tyranny of radical Islam.

During the 1990s, America's flaccid response to a number of terrorist attacks carried out by al-Qaeda bolstered the terrorist organization's reputation. As Osama bin Laden shrewdly observed, people saw al-Qaeda as a strong horse, and people naturally tend to back a strong horse. Our abandonment of Iraq would make radical Islamism the strongest horse in the region, if not the entire Muslim world, and would transform us in the eyes of our allies into the geostrategic equivalent of a skittish, broken-down nag ready to bolt at the slightest provocation. It is difficult to think of anything more disheartening to our allies.

Our defeat in Iraq would validate the means radical Islamists have employed in Iraq: mass murder and assassination. There is no doubt that terrorism would intensify all over the world as Islamists attempted to murder their way into power.

Our defeat in Iraq also would hand a major victory to an enemy we have been fighting since 1979: Islamist Iran. The loud chants of "Death to America!" heard at Friday prayers in Teheran are not an exercise in nostalgia by middle-aged Iranians, but an accurate summation of the regime's attitude and policy toward the United States. As we have stated earlier, Iran has long had designs on southern Iraq, where Shi'ite Muslims are in the majority. During the 1980s and 1990s, Iran supported the Supreme Council for the Islamic Revolution in Iraq, which now is a major political player and the sponsor of the Badr Brigade militia. Almost immediately after the liberation of Iraq in 2003, cadres from Iran's ministry of intelligence and security and its Revolutionary Guard Corps (a.k.a. the Pasdaran) began to infiltrate southern Iraq and, with money, weapons, and other forms of support, built up two major Shi'ite militias, the Badr Brigade and the Medhi Army. The latter is the armed force of the radical cleric Muqtada al-Sadr. It operates in Baghdad's Shi'ite neighborhoods as well as in cities in the Shi'ite-dominated provinces. These Shi'ite political parties and their militias advocate the establishment of an Islamic republic in Iraq along the lines of that in Iran. Therefore, they are quite plainly fronts for Iranian expansionism.

If we surrendered in Iraq, the Iranians would make an immediate, all-out effort to plunge southern Iraq into chaos by means of subversion, propaganda, intimidation, assassination, sabotage, and terrorism (think of Lebanon in the 1970s and 1980s). As soon as the time was right, they then would pry the region away from Iraq, either annexing it outright or establishing de facto control through proxies, as it did in southern Lebanon through Hezbollah. However Iran exercises control over it, southern Iraq would become a subsidiary of and source of wealth for the world's most dangerous Islamist regime and leading state sponsor of terrorism.

Another possible effect of an American defeat in Iraq would be the undermining of the confidence our allies in the region and elsewhere feel in the United States' promises of support. If we are willing to desert a people we liberated and, from the comfort of our own shores, watch their country slowly and painfully disintegrate, how could we expect other countries in the region to rely on us? When the confrontation with Iran occurs—and it is just a matter of time—we will need the material and diplomatic support of regional allies such as Jordan, Kuwait, Bahrain, and the United Arab Emirates. It seems doubtful that they will feel safe in joining our efforts to check Iranian adventurism if we abandon Iraq in part to Iran.

These, then, are the stakes in Iraq. That our enemies—Iran, Syria, and radical Islamists—share this assessment is evidenced by the ruthless, ceaseless campaigns of terror meant both to drive us out of Iraq and to prevent the establishment of a stable, democratic government. It is because they understand the stakes at hand that, as Iraq attempts to found a working parliamentary democracy during the next year, our enemies will throw everything they can into the fight.

In order to prevail in Iraq, we cannot consider a major reduction of U.S. forces on the ground. Currently, our forces bring combat power to the battlefield that the still developing Iraqi security forces do not yet have. The Iraqi forces are improving; indeed, some of them are quite effective. However, the "punch" American forces provide, the logistical, communications, and training capabilities, guarantee success in battle—especially any large-scale "stand-up" fights—for some time to come.

That said, the key to ultimate success in Iraq is the development of strong, well-disciplined, and well-trained Iraqi security forces. By fall 2006, Iraq's army, national guard, police, and other security forces will have 250,000 trained personnel. These courageous men and women, who daily take the fight to the enemy despite terrorists' threats and violence directed against them and their families, must continue to receive the training, support, and resources they need to safeguard Iraq.

The Iraqi security forces must have the proper equipment to execute their duties, including a substantial number of armored fighting vehicles, heavy weapons (such as artillery and mortars), and aircraft, especially helicopters. They also will need adequate communications, logistics, and maintenance capabilities. Developing resiliency within these forces will also demand strong training and professional education programs for enlisted men, non-commissioned officers, and officers. While the bulk of training and education must focus on military skills, these programs must aim to develop a strong sense of ethics and honor and foster a proper attitude toward civil-military relations throughout all ranks and grades. It might seem quaint to stress this, but Iraqi security forces must embrace an ethos of selfless service to the public. Otherwise, they will not gain the respect and confidence of the people they protect and serve. This, in time, will erode popular support for the Iraqi government.

In spite of the drumbeat of defeatism emanating from too many American politicians, journalists, and commentators, the U.S. presence must remain close to its current level. The trial of Saddam Hussein, the massive participation of Iraqi citizens in the referendum on the constitution, and the strong turnout for the Iraqi legislative elections in December 2005 are strong evidence that the Ba'athist regime will not be restored. Of course, the murder campaign by the Ba'athist diehards and the foreign terrorists is not calculated to win Iraqi citizens to their causes. As Lenin once proclaimed, the purpose of terror is to terrify—and that is exactly the purpose of these killers' acts of mass murder. Their ultimate goal, we believe, is to so weaken the Iraqi security forces, so intimidate their political opponents, and so frighten the Iraqi people that they can mount a successful coup d'etat, much as the Bolsheviks took power in the October Revolution.

In late 2005, reports surfaced that the terrorists were fragmenting and that the Ba'athists and foreign fighters were turning against each other. Coupled with the positive political developments and the rising capabilities and self-confidence of the Iraqi security forces, this news is encouraging, but is not grounds for complacency. Securing Iraq against domestic and foreign threats is necessary to nurture democratic governance and promote a civil society.

A continued strong U.S. military presence will strengthen the self-confidence of the Iraqi security forces, in that they will be sure of support if they need it. Of course, U.S. forces eventually will leave Iraq. They must, because in the end the fight for Iraq's independence and security must be an all-Iraqi fight. Ending the appearance of an American occupation is important to ensuring the security of Iraq, developing a robust sense of national pride within the Iraqi military, police, and the general population, and increasing support for the new Iraqi government. We should not determine the withdrawal of U.S. forces, however, by a chronological schedule, with a date firmly set for the last U.S. soldier to leave. Doing so will allow the terrorists and foreign powers who want a piece of Iraq to retire to the shadows and prepare themselves for a new offensive. American and Iraqi commanders must develop a plan that ties the U.S. forces' withdrawal to the achievement of certain goals related to the Iraq security forces' size, sophistication, and battlefield effectiveness. For example, U.S. forces will leave a certain area only when the Iraqi forces in the area have executed a certain number of *sustained* independent operations against domestic and foreign terrorists. In that way, when the U.S. military leaves Iraq, it will leave the country with a strong ability to maintain its sovereignty and security.

Another charge related to the Bush administration's conduct of the war has had amazing power, even though it is utterly baseless. Many people (among them more than a few who once had a claim to being serious) have scrutinized the men and women in the Bush administration's national security team and declared them a cabal of pro-Israel "neo-conservatives" (many of them Jews) who have hijacked U.S. national security policy in order to preserve the State of Israel and, more specifically, help the Likud Party retain its grip on power. Essentially, these critics argue, the war against radical Islamist terror is a cover. The real goal is to put the power of the United States and its allies at the disposal of Israeli Prime Minister Ariel Sharon and his Likud successors.

Israel is the most hated country in the Arab and Muslim world. The United States is the *second* most hated country in the Arab and Muslim world, the critics say, only because our government is Israel's chief supporter. Therefore, the solution to the pan-Islamist terror threat is simple: pry the neo-conservatives' hands off the tiller of U.S. foreign policy, adopt a pro-Arab policy on Palestine, and all will be well. If we abandon Israel, the pan-Islamists will no longer hate us.

This analysis is entirely untrue. The truth is, radical Islam's goals are not confined to the destruction of Israel, because radical Islam looks farther back into history and has far grander ambitions. Militant Islam has often been at war with the West—from the time of Mohammed, when Islam conquered Christian North Africa, to the end of the seventeenth century, when the Muslims were turned back from the gates of Vienna. Radical Islam is seeking to breathe new life into the history of Islamic jihad—a history of warfare against *all* nonbelievers. That is why the war on terror is a global war.

The first ambition of radical Islam is to remake the Muslim world in its own fundamentalist image. From Uzbekistan to Nigeria to Malaysia, from Kosovo to Morocco to Indonesia, the Muslim world will be returned to the "proper" militant Islamic religious, legal, political, and social order. National loyalties, they say, should mean nothing to Muslims; local and national customs and traditions should be discarded as "innovations"; and a harsh sharia law should be imposed. They see Westernized Muslim governments as corrupt, to be swept aside. Adherents to other religions, "infidels," will be put in their proper place—that is, into the status of second- and third-class citizens—or expelled or killed.

Ultimately, a pan-Islamic state would unite all Muslims and lead to the restoration of a great Islamic empire—recreating that time when the Prophet and his successors swept through the world. Once established, this empire could then turn its attention to the subjugation and conquest of the rest of the world, particularly the liberal West, as the Ottoman Turks did in the fifteenth, sixteenth, and seventeenth centuries.

Clerics educated in Saudi Arabia's ascetic Wahhabism preach this message in radical Islamic mosques from the Balkans to Berlin to Boston. Militant Islamist websites openly express contempt for "infidels" and boast of plans for a new Islamic empire. Pan-Islamic terror groups are setting up shop throughout Central Asia, often recruiting by force. Aside from attacking Indian Hindus, radical Islamists in Kashmir assault their fellow Muslims for such "crimes" as having a satellite TV dish. In Nigeria, sharia law is now the governing legal system in many states, and anti-Christian violence, often carried out by young men wearing T-shirts emblazoned with an image of Osama bin Laden, is on the upswing. In Southeast Asia, Muslim rebels have raided army camps in southern Thailand and the terrorist group Jemaah Islamiah, an Islamic militant group with links to al-Qaeda, has committed atrocities in Indonesia, including the October 2002 bombing in Bali that killed hundreds. Also, in Indonesia, the group Lashkar Jihad has sent men to regions with Christian minorities to agitate anti-Christian violence.

To say the least, Israel is not the issue here. Radical Islam is.

Our fight, however, is not against a religion. The vast majority of Muslims are obviously peaceable people. Our fight is against those who want to turn Islam into a terrorist creed preaching global violence and revolution.

What we can and must do is act against those regimes that train, shelter, and support the terrorists who are bent on killing us (Iran and Syria); put further pressure on Muslim states to curtail radical Islam within their own borders (Egypt, Pakistan); stop Muslim states from subsidizing intolerant religious belief around the world (Saudi Arabia); and demand, and bring about, an end to the WMD programs of rogue states (North Korea). We must declare a "no sanctuary for terrorists" policy and enforce it. The United States must be a faithful ally to those Muslim countries that openly oppose radical Islamist terror and that stand for tolerance and liberalization—like Morocco, Qatar, and Bahrain. Through a robust program of public diplomacy and broadcast information, the United States must promote economic, political, religious, and social freedom throughout the entire Muslim world and refute the myths about the nature of American society, politics, and culture that are rife in that world. The Five Freedoms that we've enumerated are the place to start.

In the almost two and a half years since the attacks that brought this war to our soil, the United States has brought down two bloodstained regimes of the Web of Terror. We did not fight these wars to win the next Israeli general election for Likud or even to ensure Israel's continued existence, although victory will, we hope, ensure that Israel does survive: It has that right in international law, and it is an outpost of democracy in an oppressed part of the world.

The war on terror is not a matter of law enforcement, as some politicians still seem to think. It is a war that we fight against a totalitarian ideology, like Communism, that wants to destroy Western civilization. We are, in the end, fighting this war for ourselves. And it is imperative we fight it in the right way.

In the last decade we've made tremendous progress—but it is progress that has been forced upon us. Remember that many touted the trial and conviction of the men involved in the 1993 World Trade Center bombing as a major victory in the war against terrorism. It was satisfying to be sure, but it wasn't a victory. It took the attacks of September 11, 2001, to arouse America to a better understanding of the scope of the threat. Since that day—which, like Pearl Harbor, should live in infamy—federal, state, and local governments have done much to improve domestic security, and America's intelligence and law-enforcement agencies have done great work thwarting terrorist plots. The work done to provide for the internal security of the United States is welcome, but it is not enough.

After the Axis powers declared war on the United States in December 1941, the United States did not limit its response to fortifying the Hawaiian Islands, increasing antisubmarine patrols along the Atlantic Coast, and upgrading the efforts of the FBI to crack rings of domestic Axis sympathizers and capture saboteurs. Osama bin Laden has openly and repeatedly declared war on the United States. The radical Islamists see themselves in jihad against the West, and they see the United States as the leading "Crusader" power. They see moderate Muslims who wish live in peace as traitors. Backed by state sponsors of terror like Iran, they have become a global threat just as much as the National Socialists were. Though militarily puny, their dreams and their potential danger are grandiose: inflaming a billion Muslims worldwide and creating a radical Islamist empire. To that end they will cooperate with rogue states like North Korea. They will do everything they can to acquire weapons of mass destruction.

The bottom line is that they must be stopped. End their state sponsorship, and they wither. Buttress the forces of moderate Islam, encourage freedom and tolerance in Islamic societies, grant Muslims in Iraq and Iran the opportunity to vote against tyranny and the mullahs, then the radicals do more than wither, they disappear to the fringes of Muslim society. If we are to stop the spread of radical Islam, we cannot be satisfied with the conviction of a failed terrorist bomber, dismantling a terrorist cell, or freezing the bank account of a terrorist front—however necessary all these things are. To rely purely on defensive measures cedes the initiative to the radical Islamists. Instead, we need to take the battle to them.

The counteroffensives in Afghanistan and Iraq were first steps to the endgame, they are not the endgame itself. The endgame is taking down the Web of Terror entirely so that the global terror threat dissolves. We have laid out the broad parameters of an active strategy for this war. Despite the best wishes of some, the Web of Terror cannot be talked to death, no "peace process" will work, no foreign aid will suffice unless the countries involved make a commitment—as Libya has apparently done—to forgo jihad, forgo terrorism, forgo weapons of mass destruction. Countries that will not do this willingly must be compelled to do it. Terrorism and the proliferation of weapons of mass destruction are not something we have to live with; they are something that the rogue states of the Web of Terror have to live without.

The fight is not ours alone, and it is not the West's alone. American power, American persuasion, and American might can change the regimes that support the spread of radical Islamist terror and hunt down the terrorists. But ultimately it is up to the world's Muslims to make a commitment to peace, freedom, and tolerance; to determine how they will reconcile their religion with modernity; to bring their nations more effectively into the global economy. The extinguishing of radical Islam is a project for the billion-strong Islamic world. Radical Islam is a threat to that world as much as it is a threat to the West. Promoting the Five Freedoms is our strategy for the West and moderate Islam to work together against the radicals.

Secretary Rumsfeld has characterized the war on terror as a "slog," a long, hard struggle. At times, it will seem so. It might seem so already, as the daily death toll of our soldiers in Iraq rises. But in its broad lineaments, as we have outlined in this book, the Web of Terror can be taken down—and should be taken down—swiftly. The reformation of Islam could take decades, if not centuries. Bringing democracy to the region will take years if not decades. But the primary threat, state-sponsored terror and the threat of proliferating weapons of mass destruction, can be dealt with now. To act now, in fact, is to lessen future risks. As we seek to obliterate the Web of Terror and help moderate Islam defeat its enemies (and ours), we need to remember the roots and development of our own civilization, our patriotism, our core principles. We stand armed to defend the prospect that men have the right to life, liberty, and the pursuit of happiness—and that global terrorism should not cast a pall over these inalienable rights. Sir Winston Churchill put it well when he said,

> We must recognize that we have a great inheritance in our possession, which represents the prolonged achievement of the centuries; that there is not one of our simple uncounted rights today for which better men than we are have not died on the scaffold or the battlefield. We have not only a great treasure; we have a great cause. Are we taking every measure within our power to defend that cause?

This book is our own modest effort to rally "every measure within our power to defend that cause" of peace, freedom, and prosperity.

PART FOUR

COUNTERING TERROR WITH NUCLEAR DETERRENCE

CHAPTER NINE

HOW TO PREVENT THE IRANIAN NUCLEAR NIGHTMARE

I RAQ IS THE "CENTRAL FRONT" IN the global war on terror, but it is not the only front.

Iran is openly pursuing the development of nuclear weapons (and the ballistic and cruise missiles to deliver them). It is the chief sponsor of Islamist terror, harbors al-Qaeda and other terrorists, and indirectly supports al-Qaeda's bloody campaign in Iraq. It controls the Hezbollah political-military movement in Lebanon. It has turned Syria into a client state. It dominates the Palestinian Authority after the resounding victory of Hamas in the January 2006 elections in the Gaza Strip and Palestinian areas in the West Bank. It supports the Badr Brigade and Mahdi Army in Iraq. It has a long record of meddling in the domestic politics of Afghanistan and Pakistan. And it has threatened Israel with annihilation.

Iran's president is Mahmoud Ahmadinejad. He served in the Revolutionary Guard and is assumed to be one of the "students" who took over the U.S. embassy in Iran in 1979. He is an avowed enemy of the United States, an Islamic radical, and shares the hard-liners' belief in repressing true democracy in Iran and spreading radical Islamism abroad.

Very troubling is how far afield Iran is spreading its influence. Over the last few years, Iran has begun to cultivate close relationships with the two most anti-American regimes in Latin America: Cuba and

Venezuela. The relationship between the Marxist-Leninist, officially atheistic dictatorship of Fidel Castro with the hard-line Islamists of Iran may seem odd. But Castro has been casting about for a deep-pocketed sponsor ever since the demise of the Soviet Union. Now, he has two: Iran and Venezuela, both rich with oil and natural gas, both swimming in cash, both fanatically anti-American. Cuba has nothing to offer in trade except itself: a key base for operations against the United States.

Hugo Chavez's regime in Venezuela is even more deeply involved with the Iranians. There is no economic reason for the relationship. According to a recent BBC report, Venezuela sits on an estimated 78 billion barrels of oil. If it pumps this oil at the current rate of 3.3 million barrels a day, then its reserves will last about 75 more years. If the price of oil stays between $50 and $60, then the Venezuelan oil industry will generate $165 million to $198 million a day or $60.2 billion to $72.3 billion a year (in current dollars).

Chavez shares Iran's strident anti-Americanism and support of terrorism. Venezuela shelters, arms, and supports the Revolutionary Armed Forces of Colombia (FARC) and the Colombian National Liberation Army (ELN). Both are Marxist-Leninist narco-terrorist groups that threaten Colombia. Chavez has visited Iran and met Iranian organizations that promote terrorism. Reportedly, Venezuelan paramilitaries are training with Iran's Revolutionary Guard Corps. The Revolutionary Guard Corps and Iran's ministry of intelligence and security train, organize, arm, fund, and otherwise support terrorist groups in the Middle East, South Asia, and Central Asia. Perhaps South America is now included, making Venezuela a possible base for Islamist terrorism in the Western Hemisphere.

What makes Iran even more worrisome is its ardent embrace of a 1,400-year-old Shi'ite dogma about the return of the Twelfth Imam, al-Mahdi or "the Madhi." (It is from this figure that Muqtada al-Sadr's militia in Iraq takes its name). According to the *hadith*, Muslim sacred texts that incorporate traditions and sayings associated with the prophet Mohammed, this imam disappeared in 941. He will return in apocalyptic conditions: widespread natural disasters—including epidemics—and merciless wars of conquest in which Islamic armies conquer millions and convert the vanquished to Islam. Many Iranian leaders believe they are advancing the reappearance of the Mahdi. Some Iranian clerics have claimed that the tsunamis that swept Southeast Asia in late 2004, the hurricane-caused devastation in the United States in the summer of 2005, and the earthquake that wracked Pakistan in 2005 are evidence of the imam's imminent return. Some members of President Ahmadinejad's inner circle—and Ahmadinejad himself—claim that a halo of light appeared around him when he addressed the United Nations in September 2005, making plainly evident his divine purpose on Earth.

Some might chuckle, albeit nervously, at Ahmadinejad's belief in his divine raison d'etre, but if he obtains the nuclear weapons to make his apocalyptic fantasies reality, none of us will be laughing. So we must check Iran's nuclear and terrorist ambitions.

In Iraq, for example, the Iraqi army needs to seal its borders with Iran as an act of self-preservation. The United States needs to affirm, publicly, to Iraq, Pakistan, Bahrain, Kuwait, and Qatar that we will defend them against any Iranian subversion or attack. And the U.S. Navy needs to maintain a major presence in the Arabian Sea and Persian Gulf. To paraphrase Oliver Cromwell, warships often are a nation's best ambassadors.

We must also do everything we can to revive democratic opposition groups in Iran. Through diplomacy, we must work to isolate the Iranian regime and encourage its domestic opponents. And we must consider supporting the creation of an armed resistance movement.

The stakes are high. And if Iran succeeds in developing and deploying nuclear weapons, we will have to counter with a Cold War standby: a "nuclear umbrella." That is, we need to bring our allies in the region under our protective nuclear umbrella, and announce a doctrine of nuclear retaliation against any nuclear strike against the United States or any of our allies. Nuclear deterrence is not out of date: it will be our necessary strategic doctrine against Iran and North Korea.

The Bush administration should promulgate a new strategy, "Deterrence against Nuclear Terrorism," a strategy in which we should ask our allies and other nations to participate. It might surprise some to know this, but France already has moved in this direction. On January 19, 2006, French president Jacques Chirac announced that France was prepared to launch a nuclear strike against any country that sponsors a terrorist attack against French interests. Give France's determination to use nuclear weapons in its defense, it should be relatively easy to get Great Britain to commit to such a policy as well.

President Bush should make a similar announcement in public, stating that, in this age of terrorism, the United States will hold nation-states that support terrorism and develop weapons of mass destruction to a very high standard of responsibility. Privately, President Bush should tell Iran and North Korea that the United States will meet any nuclear, chemical, radiological, or biological attack with a swift nuclear response—without waiting for confirmation of Iranian and North Korean involvement. Put another way, nations that develop weapons of mass destruction and support terrorists will be at the top of our target list. To get off that list, Iran would need to stop developing fissile material, give the International Atomic Energy Agency unambiguous inspection rights, turn over al-Qaeda operatives in Iran to the United States, and cease its support of terrorist groups such as Hezbollah, Hamas, and Palestinian Islamic Jihad.

Should deterrence fail and an enemy launch a "decapitation strike" against our government, killing the president and other leaders, our enemies should know that they will be the targets of a strategic option called "Assured Response Against Nuclear Terrorism" that will ensure preplanned nuclear strikes without further orders or warnings against them. As practiced in the Cold War, our nuclear forces should be on fifteen-minute alert status, as necessary, ready to hit programmed targets.

Certainly, some will recoil from the idea of the United States making—or, in some cases, restating—such a policy. They will accuse us of "thinking the unthinkable." To that accusation, we respond, "Guilty as charged." But it is the only way to give Iran, North Korea, and other terrorist nations a real incentive to put the WMD genie back in the bottle.

Another necessary step in developing a credible nuclear deterrent in the War on Terror will be the development of a new generation of nuclear weapons, smaller and of lower "yield," that can penetrate hardened targets such as caves or other weapons storage facilities difficult to destroy with conventional weapons. We need a nuclear "one shot-one kill" capability to take out enemy installations. Certainly, many people—in Congress, in the news media, and on the political left—will profess shock at upgrading our nuclear capability. But nuclear weapons deterred the Soviet Union, and their role of nuclear weapons has not declined in importance.

So great is the potential danger poised by an aggressive and nuclear-armed Iran, so unsettling is the prospect of its leaders with their fingers on the button, however, that the only surefire solution to the problem of Iran is regime change. To that end, the United States must immediately start planning an integrated campaign against the Iranian regime—and execute it as soon as possible. Does that mean a repeat of Operation Iraqi Freedom, with mechanized divisions smashing their way into Tehran? No. We mean an air campaign using hundreds of strike aircraft to destroy Iran's nuclear weapons facilities and its capacity to defend itself, as well as armed support of Iran's democratic resistance to overthrow the "mullahocracy."

American diplomats and political leaders must persuade as many regional governments as possible to help in this campaign, if only to lend their tacit support. As countries like Saudi Arabia, Jordan, the United Arab Emirates, Bahrain, Turkey, Egypt, and Kuwait all have something to gain from the end of the regime in Tehran, this may not be as hard of a sell than some might think. We also should ask the

United Kingdom, France, and our NATO allies to be part of the coalition. If they join, the coalition will gain high-quality forces while diplomatically and politically isolating countries that might wish to meddle, such as Russia and China.

As we mentioned earlier, one of the failings of the Iraq campaign was the reluctance of the U.S. military to recruit, train, and develop free Iraqi forces. We need to work *now* to help develop a military resistance movement within Iran. U.S. special operations forces need to infiltrate the country and prepare cadres, just as Allied agents worked to assist the French resistance in World War II. We can also train Iranian expatriates in friendly countries to insert into Iran. They would be responsible for small-scale military operations against regime targets like railroads, oil pipelines, and military communications systems. Our reconnaissance systems—satellites, electronic surveillance, signals intelligence, unmanned aerial vehicles (UAVs)—could ensure that the free Iran forces hit serious targets and do real damage. These raids would put the regime off balance, chip away at its military strength, and inspire its domestic enemies—the Iranian people who want freedom and real democracy.

The Iranian regime has been at war with the United States since 1979. It has bankrolled the killing of Americans. It has threatened our allies with destruction. We have no qualms about taking down the regime. After the free Iranian guerilla attacks would come a ferocious twenty-four-hour air attack—using more than sixty of the Air Force's stealth aircraft—B-2s, F-117s, and F-22s backed by five hundred other strike aircraft, all of them armed with precision-guided weapons. This air attack would destroy or neutralize the Iranian air force and air-defense system and attack the regime's leadership and the Revolutionary Guard Corps. It would also hit Iran's missile forces as well as all official radio and television stations. The free Iranian forces—and our media capabilities, including the Air Force's "Compass Call" aircraft—would broadcast to the Iranian people that their day of deliverance had come.

With the Iranian air-defense system and air force wiped out, our strike aircraft would be able to linger over the battlefield and take out targets with impunity. As we did in the Iraq campaign, the Air Force and Navy would establish "kill boxes" where enemy units could be smashed from the air. It would not take long to demoralize even the most committed fighters of the Revolutionary Guard Corps if we hit them relentlessly with air power as the Iranian people are rising in the streets.

The psychological pressure brought to bear against the regime would be unremitting. We would make frequent announcements that U.S. intelligence was tracking the leaders by whatever communications devices they were using (which probably not be too far from the truth) and that missile-firing UAVs and U.S. special operations forces were on their trail. U.S. forces in Iraq would make demonstrations along the Iran–Iraq border—and, then, if Iraq grants permission, the occasional incursion over the border. U.S. Navy and Marine Corps amphibious units would enter the Persian Gulf and begin to conduct raids along Iran's coast and, using various deception techniques, the U.S. Army would create and operate "phantom units" along Iran's border with Afghanistan and Pakistan. These actions would create the illusion (some of which would become reality) that U.S. and allied units could descend on Iran from any direction and at any time.

But while our troops would threaten the regime, we do not imagine the "thunder runs" of the Iraq War or a major U.S. Army presence on the ground. A closer model would be Afghanistan, where we relied heavily on local forces opposed to the regime. We expect that through our air and naval power, our occasional Marine and infantry strikes, and the armed domestic opposition led by the free Iranians, that the Iranian army and the Revolutionary Guard Corps would be beaten psychologically.

During the Iraq War, a radio news journalist found an Iraqi Republican Guard officer in the hospital. He was uninjured physically, but he was in shock psychologically, telling the reporter that there was nothing, nothing, that the Iraqi army could do to stop the Americans. *Nothing.* As soon as that attitude spreads through the ranks of Iran's army, security forces, and police, they will be finished, and the regime of the mullahs will be finished as well.

Would Iran experience a sustained terror campaign like the one the jihadists and Ba'athists are conducting in Iraq? Yes. We expect so, but the circumstances will be far different. First, there will be few American forces on the ground. Iranians will liberate Iran, and there will be no grounds for a campaign to expel the infidels. The Iranian regime's loyalists will have to call for terror attacks against their fellow Iranians, and the Iranians are not as religiously divided as the Iraqis are.

Moreover, Iran and Syria support the Iraqi insurgency. Iran's neighbors—Turkey, Pakistan, Iraq, Saudi Arabia, Afghanistan, Russia—would have no incentive to support a pro-mullah insurgency in Iran. With the exception of Syria, Hamas, and Hezbollah, the nations of the Middle East would cheer the mullahs' downfall.

Of course, the campaign to impose regime change on Iran would be risky. It would demand resolute leadership and unflinching courage from the U.S. government, as well as a willingness to see the task in Iran to its end. If, however, the United States brings such characteristics to the fight, it has every chance of being successful. And considering the risk that the mullahs pose to the region and the world as the leaders of the Web of Terror, we have every reason to fight and win this battle.

AFTERWORD

WE HAVE PURPOSELY WRITTEN this book as a military assessment and tried to keep politics out of our analysis as much as possible. But we are frankly appalled at how all too many politicians have apparently forgotten the horror of September 11, and the proper lessons of our victories in Afghanistan and Iraq. The United States is the primary target of the Web of Terror. But we can—and must—take the Web of Terror down.

In the Democratic primaries, all the candidates except Senator Lieberman disavowed the global war on terror. They tried to deny that the Web of Terror exists. They argued that our only enemy is al-Qaeda. But where does al-Qaeda live? In how many nations are its terror cells embedded? From where does al-Qaeda draw its support?

We have provided the answers in this book.

Unfortunately, not everyone wants to face the answers. For example, France, Russia, Germany, and the United Nations were all complicit in trying to keep Saddam Hussein in power. For the Europeans, Saddam was a trading partner. For the United Nations, he was a cash cow. We now have records documenting that 270 companies, organizations, and individuals in fifty countries benefited from the UN-operated Oil-for-Food program in Iraq; for them, the continuation of sanctions and Saddam Hussein in power meant the continuation of a substantial flow of money. Anyone who suggests that we should have waited for United Nations approval to remove Saddam Hussein is effectively saying that the world would be a better place with Saddam Hussein still in power in Iraq.

The benefits of removing Saddam Hussein are now flowing in. Libya has renounced weapons of mass destruction and expressed its desire for reconciliation with the West, and is even discussing possible peace talks with Israel. Pakistan has started to confess, investigate, and stop its nuclear weapons proliferation to Iran, Libya, and North Korea, and has announced peace talks with India. Iran's reformist-minded majority is growing ever more bold and defiant against the tyrannical mullahs. Syria has made tentative steps toward cooperation with the West. The list of benefits that have come from toppling Saddam Hussein continues to grow. But let's not be complacent, as Iran's rush to develop a nuclear weapons capability before our presidential elections is a major threat to the U.S. and to stability in the region.

There is still tough fighting ahead in Iraq and Afghanistan. But the jihadists know they are losing. In February 2004, a memo came to light that appears to be written by Abu Mus'ab al-Zarqawi, a terrorist affiliated with al-Qaeda and now in Iraq, to al-Qaeda's high command. In that memo, he writes, "We can pack up and leave and look for another land, just like it has happened in so many lands of jihad. Our enemy is growing stronger day after day, and its intelligence information increases. By God, this is suffocation!" The main battle is in Iraq, and al-Qaeda is losing it.

The Web of Terror will want to influence America's presidential elections because the Web of Terror will not survive four more years of George W. Bush. When critics of the war in Iraq say that Iraq will become "another Vietnam," we reply that will happen only if antiwar politicians achieve the power to make it so and appease the Web of Terror.

We have written this book to inform America of the dangers and opportunities ahead. Let us be united when it comes to guaranteeing our nation's security and eliminating the Web of Terror. Preserving American lives should not be a partisan issue.

REPORTING FROM THE SCENE

WE HAD THE OPPORTUNITY to meet with important leaders of the Middle East, including Lt. General Shaul Mofaz, Israel's minister of defense, and his royal highness, Reza Pahlavi, son of the former shah of Iran.

Our visit to Israel in July 2003, organized by the AIFL (America-Israel Friendship League), has been critical to our understanding of why the "roadmap to peace" will not succeed unless Iran, Syria, and Saudi Arabia stop funding terror. As long as Hamas, Hezbollah, and other major terrorist groups are funded and led from this Web of Terror, peace is impossible—something one sees readily on the ground in the Middle East.

We also went on the scene to Iraq in September 2003, at the invitation of Secretary of Defense Donald Rumsfeld and saw for ourselves the extraordinary progress our troops have made not only to free the country but to rebuild it.

October 9, 2002: **Note: For security reasons, the face of the man in the
center is obscured.** As the possibility of liberating Iraq was looming, Lt.
General Shaul Mofaz (left), the then-retired chief of staff of the Israeli
defense forces, met in Washington, D.C., with Lt. General Tom McInerney
to discuss war plans for potential operations in Iraq. Here General Mofaz
expressed his concerns about chemical or biological attacks on Israel and
the possibility that Israel would be drawn into the war by such attacks.
Fortunately, Lt. General McInerney's prediction of a quick victory (less
than thirty days), followed by no major urban warfare in Baghdad and no
WMD attacks on Israel, came true. They also discussed the urgency of
dealing with the potential of a nuclear-armed Iran and the danger this
presented not only to Israel, but to the world. Within weeks of this meeting, General Mofaz became Israel's minister of defense.

On January 4, 2004, Minister of Defense Mofaz publicly declared that
Iran's nuclear capabilities presented the gravest ever danger to Israel's
survival. His remarks were echoed by General Meir Dagan, chief of the
Mossad (Israeli intelligence service), in an unprecedented meeting with the
Knesset foreign affairs and defense committee.

Note: For security reasons, the face of the man on the right is obscured. Reza Pahlavi (center), the former crown prince of Iran, and Lt. Gen. McInerney met to discuss the growing nuclear threat that Iran is presenting to stability in the region. His wise advice is used throughout this book. He has our best wishes that he help lead a free and democratic Iran.

Maj. Gen. Paul Vallely; Col. Jack Jacobs, MSNBC News military analyst; and Lt. Gen. Tom McInerney meet during their July 7–13, 2003,
visit to Israel.

Ra'anan Gissin, spokesman for Prime Minister Sharon, briefs Maj. General Vallely, Lt. Gen. McInerney, and Col. Jacobs on the current status of the
"roadmap to peace."

(Seated L to R), Lt. General McInerney, Maj. General Vallely, and Col. Jacobs, are briefed by Nezah Mashiah, head of the Seam Line Project (Israel's security wall) and other Israeli Defense Force personnel.

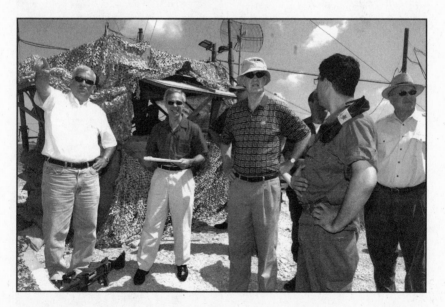

(L to R) Nezah Mashiah, Col. Jacobs, Lt. General McInerney, an Israel Defense Force (IDF) Lt. Col., and Maj. General Vallely view the security wall at a West Bank checkpoint.

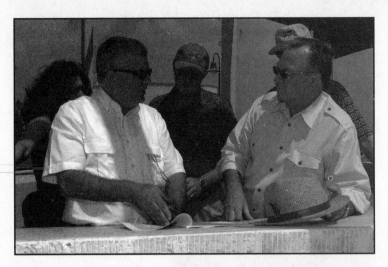

Nezah Mashiah and Maj. General
Vallely discuss the construction of
Israel's security fence. In the center
is Bill Behrer, AIFL director of communications, who hosted the visit of
the military analysts.

This picture shows a State Department official (who was responsible
for documenting the mass graves in
Iraq) standing in front of the graves
of 400,000 dead near Hila. There
have been more than 30,000 such
mass graves discovered to date.

Mass gravesite near Hila, Iraq,
that contained 3,000 Shi'ite men,
women, and children. The horrific
evidence of the mass graves alone
justified Operation Iraqi Freedom.

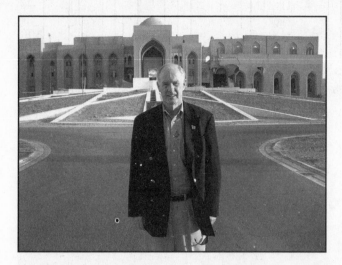

Lt. General McInerney in front of the coalition provisional authority
headquarters in the Green Zone prior to going downtown to the FOX News
Channel studios in Baghdad. Note that the right wing of the palace has no
roof, yet the rest of the building is fully operational. Smart bombs work!
September 22, 2003.

(L to R) Maj. General Viggers, British Army deputy commander; Lt. General
Sanchez, US Army commander CJTF7; and Col. Hicks, US Army J-3 CICS; brief
Lt. General McInerney and other military analysts at coalition provisional
authority headquarters September 2003.

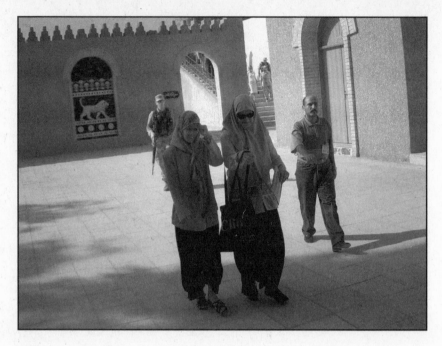

Two unidentified female guides were thrilled to show our group the magnificently restored ancient city of Babylon during our September 20–25, 2003,
visit to Iraq, as part of the first group the secretary of defense sponsored to
visit Iraq.

Ishtar Gate (replica) in Babylon, Iraq. The original is in the Pergamon Museum
in Berlin. Saddam Hussein restored this magnificent gate as part of his efforts
to restore the monuments and artifacts of ancient Babylon. One hour south of
Baghdad near the town of Hila, it will make a wonderful tourist attraction in
the coming years.

Lt. General McInerney and Maj. General Vallely stand in front of a map of ancient
Babylon after a tour of the site on September 23, 2003.

(L to R) Maj. General Vallely; Maj. General Tyszkiewicz, Polish commander of the multinational division (MND), and Lt. General McInerney pose during our visit to the MND in September 2003. The MND was replacing the 1st Marine Division, which was rotating back to the U.S.

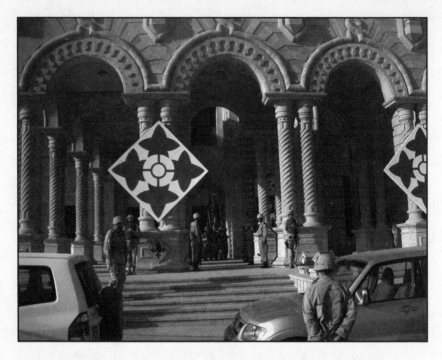

Maj. General Ray Odierno standing on the extreme left in front of his 4th
Infantry Division headquarters in Tikrit, Iraq. This palace complex, the largest
in Iraq, includes more than 170 buildings. The UN's Oil-for-Food Program
helped support such extravangances.

Old Glory flies in a C-130 transport aircraft flown by the Air National Guard. In the field, our National Guard and Reserve forces are indistinguishable from the regulars and are playing a vital role in our success in Iraq.

ACKNOWLEDGMENTS

WE BOTH FEEL TRULY BLESSED TO have had the opportunity to write a book that we believe is so important to the future of America. Obviously we owe a great debt of gratitude to many people and many organizations that each played a part in our role as military analysts.

We owe a thank-you to the FOX News Channel team and contributors, Roger Ailes, Brit Hume, Tony Snow, Bill O'Reilly, Neil Cavuto, Sean Hannity, Alan Colmes, Greta Van Sustren, John Gibson, Linda Vester, Rita Cosby, Geraldo Rivera, Steve Doocy, E. D. Hill, Brian Kilmeade, David Asman, Jon Scott, Julian Phillips, Juliet Huddy, Lauren Green, Bob Sellers, Eric Shawn, Laurie Dhue, Molly Henneberg, Kelly Wright, Jim Angle, Jerry Burke, Brian Wilson, Bret Baier, Ken "The Brain Room" Dudonis, Marty Ryan, Matt Singerman, Kevin Magee, John Moody, Shepard Smith, Mike Jerrick, Gregg Jarrett, Thom Bird, Bill Shine, Griff Jenkins, Jane Skinner, Dianne Brandi, Kiran Chetry, Patti Ann Browne, Bridget Quinn, Page Hopkins, Dari Alexander, Judge Andrew Napolitana, Rich O'Brien and the FOX graphics department, Amy Burkholder, the FOX booking staff, producers, directors, makeup departments, and the remainder of the FOX team, whose behind-the-scenes efforts come together to make each show a success.

We would like to particularly give our gratitude to talk-show hosts John Batchelor and Paul Alexander of WABC of New York; Alan Nathan, Jane Silk, Greg Corombus, and Blanquita Cullum of RadioAmerica; John Stokes of K600, Kalispell, Montana; Erich "Mancow" Muller of Q101 of Chicago; and Monica Crowley of WABC NY.

Also thanks to Charles Krauthammer, Bill Kristol, Fred Barnes, Mort Kondracke, Juan Williams, and Jim Woolsey.

A special thank-you goes to Oliver North for writing the introduction and for the opportunity to guest on his radio show many times. In particular we would like to thank him for his dedication to this country and for going back into the combat zone at this stage of his life, exposing himself to great risk during Operation Iraqi Freedom. His insights and battlefield reports as an embedded reporter were invaluable to our analysis.

We would also like to thank who we call our "first embedded reporter in Afghanistan," Steven Harrigan. And thanks to Greg Kelly and Rick Leventhal, the first embedded reporters in Iraq. Also to Jennifer Griffin in Jerusalem; Steve Centanni, James Rosen at the White House, Kelly Wright, Major Garrett, Wendell Goler, Jim Angle, Bill Tobin, Bob Armfield, Mark "Bubba" White, Bill Gertz, Rowan Scarborough, Frank Gaffney, and Jed Babbin.

A special acknowledgment to Scott Belliveau, our writer, who spent countless weeks and months working with us on this prodigious task. It could not have been done without him and we are deeply grateful.

And thanks to Marji Ross, president of Regnery Publishing, for giving us this opportunity, and to our editors, Harry Crocker and Miriam Moore, who worked so closely with us as we went to final production.

And finally, we would like to thank our other fellow military analysts, Captain (USN Ret) Chuck Nash, Lt. Col. Bill Cowan, Col. David Hunt, Maj. Bob Bevelacqua, Maj. General Burt Moore, Maj. General Bob Scales, Lt. Col. Bob McGinnis, Lt. Col. Tim Eads, Command Sgt. Major Steve Greer, Don Edwards, Dennis Ross of Mansoor Ijaz Radio,

Mark Ginsberg, Entifadh Qanbar, Tim Trevane, General Najeb al Salhi, Avi Ben-Abraham, and Waria al Salhi.

FOR FURTHER READING

See No Evil: The True Story of a Ground Soldier in the CIA's Counterterrorism Wars, by Robert Baer (Crown Publishers, 2002)

Sleeping with the Devil: How Washington Sold Our Soul for Saudi Crude, by Robert Baer (Crown Publishers, 2003)

Why We Fight: Moral Clarity and the War on Terrorism, by William J. Bennett (Regnery Publishing, 2003)

Brighter Than the Baghdad Sun: Saddam Hussein's Nuclear Threat to the United States, by Shyam Bhatia and Daniel McGrory (Regnery Publishing, 2000)

The Lessons of Terror: A History of Warfare Against Civilians, by Caleb Carr (Random House, 2003)

Terrorism, Afghanistan, and America's New Way of War, by Norman Friedman (Naval Institute Press, 2003)

A Peace to End All Peace: Creating the Modern Middle East, 1914–1922, by David Fromkin (Henry Holt, 1989)

Breakdown: How America's Intelligence Failures Led to September 11, by Bill Gertz (Regnery Publishing, 2002)

Hatred's Kingdom: How Saudi Arabia Supports the New Global Terrorism, by Dore Gold (Regnery Publishing, 2003)

Carnage and Culture: Landmark Battles in the Rise to Western Power, by Victor Davis Hanson (Anchor, 2002)

An Autumn of War: What America Learned from September 11 and the War on Terrorism, by Victor Davis Hanson (Anchor, 2002)

The War against the Terror Masters: Why It Happened, Where We Are Now, How We'll Win, by Michael A. Ledeen (St. Martin's Press, 2002)

Legacy: Paying the Price for the Clinton Years, by Rich Lowry (Regnery Publishing, 2003)

Transformation Under Fire: Revolutionizing How America Fights, by Douglas Macgregor (Praeger Publishers, 2003)

Losing Bin Laden: How Bill Clinton's Failures Unleashed Global Terror, by Richard Miniter (Regnery Publishing, 2003)

War Stories: Operation Iraqi Freedom, by Oliver North (Regnery Publishing, 2003)

The Crusaders, by Regine Pernoud (Ignatius Press, 2003)

Beyond Baghdad: Postmodern War and Peace, by Ralph Peters (Stackpole, 2003)

Taliban: Militant Islam, Oil, and Fundamentalism in Central Asia, by Ahmed Rashid (Yale University Press, 2000)

Jihad: The Rise of Militant Islam in Central Asia, by Ahmed Rashid (Yale University Press, 2002)

What Were the Crusades?, by Jonathan Riley-Smith (Ignatius Press, 2003)

Yasir Arafat: A Political Biography, by Barry Rubin and Judith Colp Rubin (Oxford University Press, 2003)

Fighting Back: The War on Terrorism from Inside the Bush White House, by Bill Sammon (Regnery Publishing, 2002)

The March Up: Taking Baghdad with the 1st Marine Division, by Ray L. Smith and Bing West (Bantam, 2003)

The Mystery of Capital: Why Capitalism Triumphs in the West and Fails Everywhere Else, by Hernando de Soto (Basic Books, 2000)

Onward Muslim Soldiers: How Jihad Still Threatens America and the West, by Robert Spencer (Regnery Publishing, 2003)

Boots on the Ground: A Month with the 82nd Airborne in the Battle for Iraq, by Karl Zinsmeister (Truman Talley Books, 2003)

INDEX